HAPPINESS IS MY BIRTHRIGHT

HAPPINESS IS MY BIRTHRIGHT

Suma Kandharaj

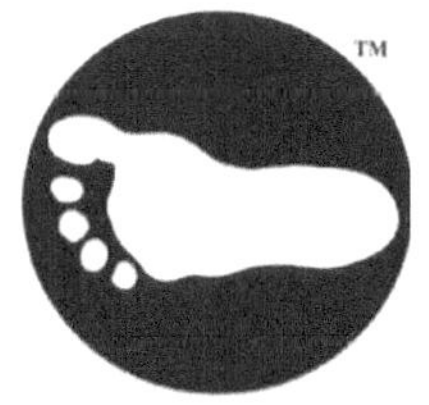

Bigfoot Publications

Because, there's a writer in everyone.

HAPPINESS IS MY BIRTH RIGHT

Author : Suma Kandharaj

First Published by
Bigfoot06 Publications (OPC) Pvt. Ltd.
211, Muzaffra, Sherpur, Pataudi,
Gurgaon, Haryana (122502)
Website: www.bigfootpublications.in
Email: info@bigfootpublications.com

First Edition: September 2022
Copyright © Suma Kandharaj

ISBN Print Book - **978-93-90925-43-8**

All rights reserved. No part of this book may be reproduced or transmitted in any form or by any means, electronic or mechanical, including photocopying, recording, or by an information storage and retrieval system—except by a reviewer who may quote brief passages in a review to be printed in a magazine, newspaper, or on the Web—without permission in writing from the copyrightowner.

Although the author and publisher have made every effort to ensure the accuracy and completeness of information contained in this book, we assumeno responsibility for errors, inaccuracies, omissions, or any inconsistencies herein. Any slights on people, places, or organizations are unintentional.

Printed in India

TABLE OF CONTENTS

Introduction

FOREWORDS

I am not a novelist or poet but Sumalatha has always encouraged me to write my experiences about my contribution to society, social life, and my business journey so far. As per her request, I have started writing my autobiography. The book's author is my second daughter and writing the foreword for the book *"Happiness Is My Birthright"* is a privilege and I convey my hearty wishes for her new journey.

42 years back…my mentor and friend Mr. Er.R. Selvaraj conveyed that when a girl child is born in the third place, the courtyard of the house will have gold spilled everywhere. My wife Vasantha, son Jawahar, daughter Anitha, the author of the book Sumalatha, father SKPP Kandasamy, mother Nagarajammal, and myself share the proud lineage of the Pandian kings who were later called the Nadans and our ancestors are from Virudhunagar.

Sumalatha's enthusiasm to write a book about her ancestors, as "The Diary of My Ancestors" created a spark in her to write this book. She took time and patience to interview and take notes from the elders in our family to collect details about their ancestral life. She has a collection of all the needed data about my ancestors from the year 1790. She was a calm girl during her schooling and though she was not a top scorer, she was appreciated by her then English teacher and present principal of VMJ School Mrs. Pearl Premkumar for her efficiency in taking notes and she did have a good opinion on her always. With the foundation from VMJ School, she got her bachelor's degree from Lady Doak College and once her children joined VMJ School, she worked as a teacher, involving herself in all the activities remembering the student's happiness and mental health as the priority. Her talent exploded once she started the TAIS academy of art and mental health to reach more students with art and counseling. In spite of being a mother of three and taking care of her family, the way she juggled so many activities gave me pride and contentment as her father. Her care, concern, and role in the life of so many people are commendable.

The book *"Happiness is my birthright"* throws light on her life, challenges, and the elegant way how she won every rising tide by encasing her with happiness and positivity to continue her journey by brightening the path of many! I acknowledge Sumalatha's strong belief in living a happy life realizing it as everyone's birthright in spite of the toughest days and moments.

-SKPPK Vasanthavel

My wife does things to make herself happy. One such initiative is this book. I am truly inspired and happy to read her work as her spouse. She always discusses the ideas with me before penning down those. Amidst her tight schedule of raising our 3 children, she took the great initiative of publishing this book. Also, she is a multitasker, a great mother, spouse, teacher, artist, counsellor, therapist and now an "Author". I am gifted to have her by my side as my spouse.

-Kandharaj Johnson

Suma is my younger sibling and I take immense pride in sharing my thoughts about how amazingly she has sculpted herself as a wonderful human being down these years. I recollect and treasure our cherishing memories growing up together. Her positive attitude, motivating pep talks and warm heart made her reach many hearts.

I have seen her perform different roles as a good daughter, daughter-in-law, sister, wife, mom, soft skill trainer, teacher, and now a writer who inspires all of us. I have always adored her patience and perseverance in every task. Her thoughts and ideas are inked as words in this book *"Happiness Is My Birthright"*. This book will reach out and capture so many minds to do their best and make them the best version of themselves.

My best wishes and prayers for her wonderful journey as an author and of course looking forward to many more surprises!

-Anitha

Happiness is the most priceless gift from God to each one of us. I am the sister-in-law of this book's author. I am glad to pen a few words about this wonderful person. She is a person of compassion and care. She is very optimistic and always looks at the silver lining of clouds. She has a secret mantra of living her life happily with ample energy. Reading this book will surely help you find happiness and attain this secret mantra.

-Preeta Jawahar

I got introduced to this book's author Suma during my childhood days. She is my cousin! Every now and then we need that little motivation to keep going in our life and we all have our own way of getting it. My sister's inspiring ways of doing things, incredible energy and thought process has helped me in numerous ways. I am sure with her book *"Happiness is my Birthright"* she will help each one of us brew love and happiness in our heart.

-Suganthi

I have known Sumalatha for the past 40 years! She has been my best friend, for as far my memory goes…Seen her go through every stage of life; an affectionate daughter, a caring friend, a loving wife, a doting mother of three, a counsellor, a teacher, an artist … and now, an author! She is relentless when it comes to helping others or trying to make someone else's life better, with her never ending kindness.

To know what light is, you need to know what darkness is! To know what true happiness is, you need to know what sadness is! But sadness is not just being unhappy; sadness is the inability to find a way to happiness! That's where this book comes in… HAPPINESS IS MY BIRTHRIGHT. Here the author tells the reader what one of our most important birthright is…to be happy! Simple as it may sound, it's something one often finds difficult to master! The author has had her share of ups and downs in life, just like all of us…what makes her stand out in the crowd is the way she pulls herself up every time and decides to stand up strong and continue her pursuit of happiness!

She has a way with words, and has put together this book, which is such an eye opener. I am sure you will enjoy this work of art, and it might even change the way you look at life, in a brighter way. Happy reading!

-Dr.S.Pradeep

The Bestie!

The book's author Sumalatha is not my school friend, college friend, childhood friend, or even family friend. She came into my life unexpectedly as my son's classmate's mother. We were casual friends initially but didn't take long to become thick friends. I appreciate the way she values people, and relationships and creates bonds that last forever. I was a bit hesitant to talk to her when I got to meet her at school but she would just walk to me, converse, and eventually made this 13 years of friendship a memorable one. She did lend her shoulder to lean on and her empathetic listening was therapeutic always. I love the way she gets into my shoes and completely understands how I feel. Apart from soothing and comforting me, she suggests ways to figure out solutions as well.

Depressing days were not so harsh with her by my side. I was upset thinking my son didn't have a sibling and was worried he would be our only child. She didn't let me stay at home and brood over the thought. She distracted me from the routine and made me attend a few workshops. Once she opened her art academy, I was her first student and began with an oil painting. I was pregnant with my second child once I started painting. She is my lucky friend! Her positive thought and words did channelize me into a positive path to tune my thoughts and manifest my wish rapidly. It hasn't been just me… now my daughter counts on her when she wants to get rid of any fear related to school or teachers. I connect my daughter to my friend through calls and a 5 minutes counseling session per day helps her face her fears!

She is a selfless person when it narrows down to help. Maybe she got it from her mom who has also been moral support with her advice and healing sessions when I was terribly ill. Her help was commendable during my second pregnancy when I had to stay in bed 24/7. Having one friend like her is much the same as having 100 friends. Traveling with her through this book will not only draw positive moments into your life but you would transform yourself into a newborn dynamic personality, mentally strong enough to handle negative situations too.

I would assure the readers that once you start reading this book *"Happiness Is My Birthright "*, your life will draw positive happenings. Do not stop with just reading this book, also try to befriend her and keep her close to you so you can progress to the next stage of your life and level up. I am eager to read this book like everyone!! Happy reading!

-Pavala Meena

Sumalatha, a good friend since my school days. A versatile artist, life coach, teacher and now an author. She keeps inspiring ☺

Happiness enhances life experience and managing our mindset has a great impact in our daily lives. Happy people are healthier, wiser, more successful, live longer and the benefits go on.

This book show cases simple, yet powerful techniques for the readers in their journey to happiness. I am sure reading this can transform lives and make our world a better place.

A must have book in your home library and recommended for all ages.

-Arul Kumar Tamil Mani

It was not a surprise when Sumalatha shared her excitement that she has authored a book and it was in the stage of publishing. She requested me to pen the foreword and knowing her personally for three decades, I felt privileged. The title of her book *"Happiness is my Birthright"* reflects her radiant nature, full of radiant energy flowing through her piece of work, each chapter has its message to convey.

I have observed her through the various turning points in her life, as an adolescent student in the transition to self-sufficiency. Later, the matured outlook of a parent with family responsibilities and challenges. Life has not been a bed of roses for her but she has always bounced back to catch up with the effervescent happiness within her. There has never been a dull moment in her life as echoed by her in her writing which you will experience as you leaf through this book.

As a colleague, I have seen her artistic talent, the creativity which is the elixir of her life and she cherished every moment in the company of students...which was explicitly seen in her interaction with them. Her working space filled with colors reflected her happiness in life. She has blossomed into a spontaneous writer. *"Happiness is my Birthright"* strikes an easy reading filled with personal experiences retold in simple language. It is filled with practical suggestions to achieve happiness, if read and habit formed, it would become a secret key to happiness.

I congratulate Sumalatha for exploring the locus *"Happiness is my Birthright"*. A journey of a thousand miles starts with a simple step.

Happy Reading!

-Pearl Premkumar

Principal

To the world, Mrs. Suma Kandharaj is an artist, teacher, dancer, counselor, and writer too! But to me, she is my best chum. Life with its ebb and flow continues and we manage to establish a rapport that I hope both of us are cherishing. What made her so attached is a question unanswered.

Five years of academic life at VMJ School, Madurai would have ended but the bond between us will never. Indeed, it is my delight to have in my heart, her art as a part of nostalgia! There is magic in her teaching methodologies. During her class sessions, no wonder I become one of her students because of her stupendous attitude. Her mantra is to love her work in all things and do her best.

The writer believes in the unique blend of happiness and edutainment. This becomes her tool to discover and impart the communication skills of the global language. She also insists that there are no hard rules to reserve English for the classroom and Fine Arts for the stage. The writer keeps repeating the mysterious message in her classes- happiness is contagious. And the quintessential part is what she has achieved.

In my opinion, happiness means divinity. It is effervescent to read, "Happiness Is My Birthright". It is not easy to find the ultimate veracity but the book substantiates the inestimable value of ecstasy and the ethereal beauty of life. It is not that ephemeral bliss but you will not be baffled to experience the blessed blow of serendipity. The journey with the writer is so fetching!

Reading means a lot to me and thus so for you. Unless we open and read a book, we may not know the pleasure of reading. I am engulfed by tranquility whenever I travel on an enchanted path through books. I dare say in this book, you will discover the truth. The aurora in you will be exhilarating. You will be one with the supreme power and become jubilant. You will not forget to laud the writer and you will understand the requisite in your birth- happiness.

-Ramya N.

I got introduced to this book's author as my sister's friend's mom. I was drawn close to her by her simplicity and warm kindness that in no time she started playing her role in my life as a friend, later a guide and finally as a mom.

She was a game changer in my life. She taught me the art of self-love and showed me what true happiness is during my low key days. She has been a real motivation while I was striving hard to get through Mr. Madurai body building competition. Anytime when I had less energy both physically and mentally during practice sessions, starving myself without food… I would ask her to send voice messages which motivated me instantly and put me back on track. Her words are magical that she connects with our feelings and draws us out of pain. I have believed and felt guilty during many situations of my life thinking I was responsible for the problem. She brought me out of guilt and explained I can't be responsible for other's misunderstanding. The long walks and motivational talks before my competitions went hand in hand to mold me as a unique person and also to win the body builder title.

I want the readers to understand that she knows the importance of words and how kind her words are!! Finding people with positive vibes has become difficult these days and she is one with ample positivity and happy vibes. The best part is she absorbs the negativity and loads us with positivity. I am sure the readers are promised to find a new self after the completion of this book.

-Akash

Mrs Suma Kandharaj professionally is a teacher, artist, counsellor, dancer as well as a writer…but personally she is my life mentor. As destiny would have it, she came into my life as a soft skill instructor and now she is like a mother to me.

During every tough situation and scenario, she taught me how to make decisions. My life literally became pleasant after she entered it. I was weak in academics and my motivation level was very low during my high school days. Her magical words and genuine care for me, changed my life instantly. I was able to focus on my studies and score well in my board exams. During tough and depressed times when nobody paid heed to my problems, she was the only person who listened patiently and motivated me to overcome my depressed state. She understands our feelings, thinks from our perspective and guides us… eventually drawing us out of our pain and problems. She is a multi- talented person and is an inspiration to the people around her. Wherever I may go in my life, a part of all my success and victory will always be credited to her. Her motivational talks and loving words are the reason behind my self-motivation and enthusiastic learning skills which makes me stand unique and proud.

The readers will be able to relate to her valuable words, which are as kind and thoughtful as she is. It is challenging to find optimistic people these days, but she is one such person who absolutely radiates happiness and positivity. She is skilled to drain out ones negative energy and replace it with clarity and peace. I am certain the readers will discover a new and sharpened version of themselves by the completion of this book.

-*Rishi Varman. R.T*

PREFACE

Hi Readers!

Having been a happiness buff unfailingly, not sure if happiness tagged along or if I tagged myself with happiness ever since I have known this world! Happiness has been a source and comrade to rejuvenate me and the vibe kept me going for days or even months together. Growing up, I have been a seeker of happiness in every itty-bitty moment and episode. Traveling back to my childhood days, I remember the jiffy my parents kept me in the know about the summer trip to my grandmother's place when the train tickets were booked, a mystique happiness wave would take shape from nowhere to motivate, prepare and complete my final exams perfectly!

The hunt for happiness was lying deep down in me even as a child. As I grew up through the ups and downs of my life, I was able to surf using the happiness wave and it did give my life some sort of balance always. I didn't like low and sulky days ever and an urge to get back to my happy vibe and happy self was fruitful enough to find myself again and again at a much faster pace. Being soaked in happy vibes always, I couldn't tolerate just few hours of sulky moments. I would hate myself for the way I felt when upset. Becoming an adult, I sensed that anyone who spent some time with me was happier and also felt charged up after meeting me or visiting my home.

Stepping into the next stage of my life as a teacher, my students asked me if I never had problems in my life and how could I be so happy and cheerful always. The moment was painful and I realized the children were struggling to find happiness amidst academics and pressure from school, teachers, and parents.

I have always believed in etching a mark during this lifetime of mine. To do something worthy before it is time for me to leave was one repetitive thought. Apart from leaving a legacy of love and respect for my children and students, I wanted them to know the importance of happiness and its miraculous touch, which can help each person achieve in life, academics or whatever the individual wants to have. It was so disturbing to see people going through days and months of depression, unable to recognize it is they who create their happiness and the outside world is not responsible for it.

The most painful part is to see how people fail to realize that happiness is their birthright and happiness is the bedrock required for anything to begin with. The student's question "How are you happy always?" triggered a thought about writing a book about happiness, so everyone can realize how delightful life is, knowing about each one's right to happiness, its importance and how to keep oneself happier?

This book will aid to understand that facing pain, problems and hard times are part of life's growing process, and once you seek happiness in every moment of your life, positivity tags along too. Happiness is my birthright and everyone's birthright, be it any being or creature in this world.

DEDICATION

This book is dedicated to the seekers of happiness…

Who encouraged me to write.

ABOUT THE AUTHOR

Suma Kandharaj is a South Indian writer and happiness addict from the Temple city of Madurai. She is the founder of the TAIS Academy of Art and Mental health and juggles classes, exhibits, workshops, and counseling sessions for the past two decades. Being a motivational speaker, positive psychology practitioner, and passionate artist, her passion for art and psychology has designated her as a Therapeutic Art Life Coach.

Deciphering her life's meaning and purpose and being a mindfulness and happiness life coach, her reach during counseling sessions are prompt. It didn't take her long to realize that she has been bestowed with the gift of being a transmuter... when a stranger, friend, or family member who might be feeling sad, fearful, or just low, began to feel lighter and better when they were around her while her energetic field cleared their energy. Possessing a golden aura, she seems to be naturally happy to be alive. Her vital energy is overwhelming and awe-inspiring that wounded individuals who need guidance and advice are attracted to her. Her positivity is enormously contagious that it can truly shift the perspective of those drowning in negative rumination and emotions.

She loves to write books that can motivate and inspire one by showing light. Her writing style is simple yet power packed with lifetime events from the home, workplace and with people, which can be applied and realized in your life. She believes in humanity, compassion, loving-kindness, unconditional love, and positivity and also never fails to shower the readers with the same. Her love for children drew them closer and bridged them to bond and open up during counseling sessions and also during her journey as a teacher. She has been a favorite teacher to her students accepting her as a journal therapist, art instructor, soft skill instructor, and personality development coach.

INTRODUCTION

I was living one accustomed life as a mom of three girls, juggling my day-to-day chores like anyone else. My life was reshaped once I joined VMJ School Madurai as an English room teacher and soft skill instructor. I met the real ME, the flair hidden and the real purpose of my life. The opportunity to change the life of so many students has been the greatest gift of being a teacher.

I believe a teacher should be a second mom and I have tried to be one always with my students. It is an overwhelming sense of touch when my students call me MOM, as a replacement for MAM when my part in their life is complete and they are ready to face this world. The journey from MAM to MOM has always been the happiest one ever.

Every class hour at school begins with some random happy moment, appreciation and humor with the students because once their mood is pepped up, they are happy and ready to get the inputs from my life lesson class. It was delightful to see a few students mentioning my class as "Happy Hour". I check the happiness scale of the students before every class.

I begin with the class only after their important problems are addressed and once they feel happier. Happiness and laughter help to increase memory, learning and in fact incorporating humor into education leads to higher test scores.

I have always been a cheerful, bubbly and happy person throughout my journey, in spite of the ups and downs in my life. The very first question any student would ask is

"Don't you have any problems in your life? You seem to be happy always!"

The very thought that pained me was when the students who need to be the happiest didn't know how to keep themselves happy. Happiness derived from life's simple things were invisible to them. The input from teachers and parents had built them in such a way that they believed and told themselves,

"I can be happy only when I score the best mark or become the class topper and school topper."

This is not the case with only students but even adults don't understand happiness is a journey and not the destination. Happiness is the key used to reach their destination.

THE WRONG THEORY:

HARDWORK.....SUCCESS.....HAPPINESS

THE RIGHT THEORY:

HAPPINESS.....HARDWORK.....SUCCESS

The right theory explains that happiness must be the foundation because when at ease, one would be able to focus and progress with hard work. Hard work will eventually bear fruits and success is yours. Happiness is purely contagious. People are naturally drawn to people who are cheerful, happy and positive. Children are attracted and tend to like adults who smile at them. One has to set happiness as the first goal in life and organize all the activities around it.

This is one quote that I love and also follow:

"Your smile is your logo, your personality is your business card, and the way you make others feel is your trademark."

Good health is a result of happiness and it protects your heart, strengthens your immune system and fights stress. Happy people have fewer aches and pain. Happiness lengthens our lives and also combats disease and disability. It does increase the activity of antibodies in your body by even destroying viruses and tumor cells.

People who hunt for happiness always forget to search for it within themselves rather they search for it in the outside world.

E.g. A man asked the sculptor "How did you manage to make such a beautiful sculpture from stone?"

The sculptor replied, "The beauty is already hidden there and I chipped out the extra rocks and the sculpture revealed itself."

Your happiness is also hidden within yourself, revise your thoughts and remove the worries within to reveal the eternal happiness lying dormant inside you. You might have a few thoughts clinging to you right from your childhood like I will be happy

- When I score the best marks

- When my teacher appreciates me

- When my classmate makes friends with me

- When my classmates stop bullying me

- When I win this competition

- When I get the best group in my high school

- When I get admission to the best college

- When I get the best job

- When I get the best salary

Trust me! Happiness doesn't have anything to do with all that I have mentioned above. If u have to wait for all this to happen, well this beautiful life that you have got will end in no time. This book will help you keep up with the little happy moments that you come across, as you live your life and be amused by the blissful journey of life. Each topic that you read are the ones that you come across in your daily life and you will get to know how to extract the essence of happiness every moment of it.

Life comes around once and it is a blessing, so do whatever makes you happy and be with whoever makes you smile.

This book will make you understand happiness is a choice and not a result and that nothing will make you happy until you choose to be happy. None can make you happy unless you decide to be happy. Your happiness will not come to you but it can only come from you. The happiest people on the planet are the ones who are constantly trying to better themselves by working on ways to improve themselves, to be stronger, smarter, and more capable.

Happiness gives good physical health and your food is digested better when meals are eaten in a pleasant atmosphere with people who can make you happier. After a spell of happiness, a person looks better, his skin is clearer, has more glow and his eyes seem brighter. Happiness is contagious and magical too. Let us see how to use happiness in our life to live life to the fullest.

I can assure you…

Your happiness is just a page ahead…

HAPPY READING!

WHAT IS HAPPINESS?

Happiness is a byproduct of a few activities and is an overall experience of pleasure and meaning. Pleasant moments make us happy and make our life happier. Pleasant moments just don't happen but one can plan for more pleasant moments in daily life and day-to-day activities. Knowing the meaning of your life brings ample happiness and in fact people who know the purpose and meaning of their life are much happier.

You don't realize what you do daily can make you more or less happier. Happiness is not a goal but it is about the journey and not the end goal. Happiness is a journey!

WHAT DETERMINES HAPPINESS?

40% of our life is truly based on intentional activity and you can become happier if you decide to intentionally do things or activities. It will help you become happier. Happiness bursts out and gets contagious by having positive emotions, being in the flow, getting fully engaged and focused in the present activity, having productive relationships, having meaning in life, and also by achieving something.

1. HELPING

"If you light a lamp for somebody it will also brighten your path."

- BUDDHA

"A life not lived for others is not life."

- MOTHER TERESA

Helping someone makes you happier as the brain releases oxytocin, serotonin, and dopamine and these hormones can boost your mood right away. Volunteers and social workers with a helping hand feel stronger, energetic and feel great about themselves since they are of purpose to someone somewhere and in return they feel calmer and less depressed with an elevated feeling of self-worth. It creates a sense of possession and decreases isolation. One act of kindness over and over leads to more. The more you do for others, the more you do for yourself and that is the reason why volunteers excel in health and added happiness than non-volunteers.

Helping doesn't need to be done on a bigger scale always and does not need advertisement or any recognition. Simple acts of help done right at your home by giving breakfast for a maiden who hasn't had her meal but still sweats to keep your home clean, feeding any stray animal passing by, helping calm down a stranger who has slipped from his vehicle by offering sips of water does add meaning to your day and life eventually.

Help rendered by my daughters Isha, Ela, and Inicka to clear the dishes and arrange my kitchen after dinner is immense for me. The small help given by my girls saves my time, and maybe I get to read a few extra pages from my favorite book before bedtime. My husband Kandharaj has this routine every morning to peel and chop the fruits to make milkshakes or fresh juices. The morning hours are achingly stressful for any woman to get food on table by the right time for the school goers and office goers. That gesture of help means a lot to me in these 20 years of my married life. Children who grow up seeing their parents helping each other with home chores become understanding life partners and also volunteer to help often.

Recollecting the words of my spiritual father and Guru Rev Dr. Bhikkhu Bodhipala, "God has blessed each one of us with two hands, while one is for us, the other is to help and serve this world. The best life one can ever get is to be born as a human because you have been gifted with hands to give charity (dhanam) and the best of all dhanam is annadhanam (offering food)."

His words did make a deep impact on me and I practice helping in ways possible no matter big or small they may be - to carry some biscuit packs with me while traveling just to feed the dogs in the streets. That moment when I feed the hungry animals who are starving is pure bliss and satisfaction.

The Himalayans make sure to help someone everyday just to make it a perfect day. At the end of the day they recollect the happenings of the day and if they notice they haven't helped someone, they never go to bed but instead they would walk to the other monk's hut to offer some water or be of some help to them and only then do they go to sleep peacefully and end that particular day.

2. BEING YOURSELF

An extensive number of people sacrifice what they like to do or what they like to wear just to satisfy others and to avoid the commotion. Every time you give up being yourself, you are not the real you and are seemingly caught in the downward spiral which pulls you into the depression that breaks your self-confidence, self-esteem, and finally your birthright i.e. HAPPINESS.

Giving up being yourself happens unconsciously due to the environment, people and happenings. Most often it happens to please someone. When you change yourself to make someone else happy, you lose yourself, the original personality, your individuality, and the real YOU.

Be yourself! Let people see the real, imperfect, flawed, crazy, weird, beautiful, magical person that you are! Do not change yourself so the other people will like you but instead, be yourself so the right people will like you. Embrace your weirdness. Some will love you but others won't. Just worry about loving yourself instead of loving the idea of other people loving you.

By being yourself, you have created something wonderful that has not been before in this world. Write the story of your life yourself and never let anyone else hold the pen. Build your life the way you want it to be by being the architect of your future. Make it a goal to love yourself and your life. Capture pictures of moments with people and click pictures of everything. Never think twice to tell people that you love them. Push yourself to do things that you are scared to do because everyone has to grow old and die one day. So, never have regrets. Live your life to the fullest and never fail to make it the best story in the world!

Feel proud of who you are instead of wishing you were someone else. You seriously never know who was looking at you and wishing they were you. You have this one life. How do you want to live it? Apologizing? Questioning? Hating yourself? Dieting? Running behind people who don't see you? Do not be a coward, be brave. Believe in yourself. Do what makes you feel happier. Take challenging tasks and risks in your life. Make yourself just proud!

The relationship with yourself sets the tone for every other relationship you have. The way you treat yourself is the way you treat others. Newly married girls from Indian families lose their complete selves and transform into a different version to satisfy the people in their in-law's place. I have heard a young man talk with pride in himself that he will quickly mold his wife and change her to his expectation. I was left wondering if the girl is any kind of clay dough!! The movie "The Great Indian Kitchen" explains the concept well, where the newlywed gives up everything and finally become aware of having traded her happiness, dignity, individuality, voice, wishes, preferences, dream, goals, and finally her whole self!

If you are utterly sensible that you aren't hurting someone or ruining someone's life, well don't hesitate to be yourself. You are already born, the time to die has already been destined, and in between, you have something called life to live. You came to this world all alone and will be exiting this world alone. You have been created as yourself because you have a purpose and some need in this world. You have been created as you because the world needs you, the real you. People who do not feel happy and worthy are the ones who have changed themselves to make someone else happy and calm. Being yourself is the first step to happiness!

3. YOU ARE A MASTERPIECE

There will be moments at school, college, or even at your workplace when you are not accepted in a group. During moments like these, there is no need for you to give away your original self. Never change yourself to get recognition or so people will accept you. There is absolutely no need to lose yourself to win a relationship. You don't realize you are losing yourself to win a relationship! You will regret in the long run for giving away your real power - your unique self. Any group that doesn't accept you as your own real self or as who you really are is not your real world.

There is always a world for you, which awaits your arrival. The world where you will be pampered, crowned, and celebrated as the king or queen for just being yourself. Find that very world buddy, in fact that world will find you. Everyone has been sculpted with uniqueness to serve a purpose that can be fulfilled only by being your unique self. You as you alone can serve your purpose. You are here to be you…JUST YOU!

There can't be anyone else like you in this whole world. It is time to realize how precious you really are. Did you know that every star is important to the sky?! You are here for a special mission. You were created as you for a particular purpose. The moment you hate yourself or try to change yourself to fit in the crowd, you tend to forget the very reason for your existence and eventually forget who you really are?! The term masterpiece is derived because there can't be one more similar piece. In the same way there can be only one person like you.

You are already here as a masterpiece. You are a masterpiece of God - chiseled and sculpted so very carefully for your very presence at the right moment. Await your turn and you will be surprised to see how beautifully you would be using your real self to serve the people and the world. Never allow anything or anyone to dim the light in you. Keep it glowing and let it burn bigger and bigger because you are a MASTERPIECE!!

4. GRATITUDE

"It is not happy people who are thankful; it is the thankful people who are happy."

The power of gratitude is immense and once you know to practice gratitude in your daily life you can easily attract everything you wish for. A person who practices gratitude will never run out of food, money, people, happiness, and whatever you want will flow as avalanches into your life. Gratitude has the power to make one happier instantly. This fast world has a majority of people who complain rather than those who appreciate and are thankful for their life. People who complain about life, stress, hardship and failed relationship would attract more problems and pain into their own life. Unfortunately, they fail to understand that they are responsible for their dull dark days.

We seek God's guidance only while in trouble and pain. Have you ever noticed yourself thanking God during smooth happy days? The law of gratitude insists that the more you thank and appreciate your food, money, asset, workers, maidens, parents, teachers and friends, you will have abundance flowing in. Gratitude multiplies and gives back in abundance.

The first sip of my fresh fruit juice intake begins with thanks to the farmer who sowed the seed, watered and grew it, the wholesaler, the retailer, the fruit vendor, my mom who sent the driver to buy the fruits, the driver who brought the fruit to my doorstep, my husband who peeled it and chopped and dropped into the juicer. Each sip goes in with gratitude.

"With all my heart thank you for the healthy drink."

The drink tastes much more heavenly and you would definitely know how gifted you are to have the glass of juice when so many are starving.

The gratitude journal that I list does magic in my life. In fact, I am able to attract what I need into my life by writing a gratitude note for any 10 things each morning and it is also the best way to start the day. The moment we wake up, we are in a hurry to catch up with this fast world. We do have so many reasons to be grateful each morning -

- For being alive today,

- For being able to get on our toes,

- Our organs functioning properly,

- Can inhale and exhale effortlessly,

- For having one more day and one more chance!!

Every passing day, your life, and your existence in this very world is a miracle and it wouldn't be enough even if you thank God every moment.

This is the way I write my gratitude journal:

I am truly blessed to…

I am happy and grateful for…

I am truly grateful for…

With all my heart, thank you for…

Thank you! Thank you! Thank you!

What else can you be thankful for? Gratitude for the best maid, cook, gardener, health, workout time, fitness, peace, happiness, harmony in your life, money flow, abundance, food, clothing, the roof above your head, a loving family and obedient children. The beautiful thing about gratitude is that even when you don't have the best of the above list, by being thankful you will be able to get 100% of what you want!!!

I have this practice of attracting what I want by just being thankful and writing a gratitude note in my gratitude journal.

Anytime I have to look out for a good maid or driver, this is what goes into my journal:

With all my heart, thank you for the perfect maids who help me keep my home and make my day easier.

I am truly blessed to have the perfect driver who is humble and takes us on safe rides ever. Thank you, thank you, thank you.

So, gratitude helps manifest and attract anything that you want into your life. Don't you think it's the best happiness to get whatever you wish for? Gratitude and happiness are inseparable and you will have a better understanding once you start practicing gratitude in your daily life.

5. MINDFULNESS

The roots of mindfulness are Buddhism, Taoism, and Yoga. Mindfulness means paying attention to the present moment and that you connect yourself to the moments regardless of whether they are good or bad but accepting them just as they are. It is about accepting your life as it is and accepting yourself just as you are. It also helps to understand who you are, to increase your happiness, overall well-being and health too. Mindfulness fails or doesn't work when you don't live in the present but instead are in the past or future. The word present also has another meaning "The gift". The present is the real gift we have in our hands but one fails to look at the treasure in hand. Most of the time is spent thinking about the past or worrying the about future.

We never drive our car looking into the rearview mirror, do we? You have to look ahead and monitor the driving! What would lead to a car accident? Mindless driving! The same way, our mind spends most of the time thinking about the past and future moments missing what we are doing now.

Mindlessness: *You don't know what you are doing or did.*

Mindfulness: You exactly know what you have been doing.

Mindfulness can be applied in life by practicing breathing, meditation, and yoga. Mindfulness has marvelous side effects in life like better relationships, fewer injuries, success at work, improved health, overall wellbeing, more happiness, feeling of relaxation, reduced stress, help with difficulties, and control our anger, emotions and desires.

Years back when I attended a spiritual course from Rev Dr.Bhikku Bodhipala, the first and foremost technique to be mastered was mindful breathing known as Aana Paana Sati.

Aana means Inhalation, **Apaana** means exhalation and **Sati** means being mindful. The Buddhist technique is all about noting the inhalation and exhalation while meditating.

By being mindful about each step and feeling good about accomplishing each one, u release dopamine and dopamine makes you feel joyful instantly. Spending more time in the present moment and being more mindful can release even more dopamine. To establish a new habit you have to be mindful of the present moment. New habits like waking up early and a workout routine can make one happier and more mindful too.

How can you apply mindfulness in your day-to-day life?

1. MINDFUL LISTENING - When you are engaged in a conversation with someone, you can listen mindfully by truly paying attention, instead of thinking about what should you say next while it is your turn to talk. It happens with most of us that we don't listen to people when they converse but we think about how we should respond. Empathetic listening practiced by the counselor during counseling session is soothing because the counselor listens quietly with their heart.

2. MINDFUL WORKING - It can be combined with anything that you do at the present moment. You are prone to get hurt if you are not mindful of what you do. Walking down the stairs mindlessly can increase the chances of falling.

3. MINDFUL EATING - Great speakers who are to give a speech later, take their time during a meal by practicing mindful eating. They eat their food calmly and in silence by living that present moment to give a speech to 1000 people later. Speakers need quietness to get them ready.

4. MINDFUL WALKING - While taking a walk from home to the grocery store, walk mindfully by paying attention to what is going on and look around. You would notice things that you haven't noticed before.

5. MINDFUL LIVING - Cleaning your home helps you live in the present moment. Enjoy washing vessels, or doing laundry in the present moment. Be happy instead of complaining. Woman usually face the panic mode during the morning rush hours by thinking about the pending work or the next task to be done while doing a task already. Focus on the task at hand and enjoy doing it. Don't try to multitask because it gives stress.

6. MINDFUL BREATHING - Aanapanasati can be practiced using a few tools which would aid to concentrate better. You may practice mindful breathing by keeping your focus on your nostril by feeling the chillness while inhaling and warmth while exhaling or inhale and exhale noting the shoulder raising and going down or by noting your belly raise while inhaling and your belly flat while exhaling.

6. PEOPLE, BONDING AND RELATIONSHIP

People and relationships are quite mysterious since they have the potential to make someone's life or ruin the whole lifetime. It is all about learning to hold on to the best ones and slit the toxic ones but unfortunately, most of us are unaware of who is who!?

We are often let down by the most trusted people and loved by the most unexpected ones.Strive hard to be that unexpected one in everyone's life. Some make us cry for things that we haven't done, while others ignore our faults and just see our smiles. Some leave us when we need them the most, while some stay with us even when we ask them to leave. The world is a real mixture of people. We just need to know which hand to shake and which hand to hold after all. That is life - learning to hold on and learning to let go!

Relationships are remarkably precious and ensure you don't lose one just because of ego and misunderstanding. Hurting someone consciously or unconsciously by words or actions does leave a permanent mark. The nail pinned to a fence can be removed but the mark or hole it leaves is standing and irreversible. It just takes a moment to hurt people you love but it takes years to heal.

My family has set eyes on people who have deliberately hurt me - the people for whom I have been during difficult times and helped. In spite of whatever resulted, they have always seen me forgive, sort out the issue and get back on good terms with them.

The question from their side has always been WHY?

And it has had my standard answer, "I don't want to neglect anybody with whom I was angry and hadn't forgiven when it is time to leave this world." Getting back to terms with them makes the relationship stronger than before and after winning them back, I have a special place in their heart ever. The power of kindness is enormous! When someone is rude, show them love and if they are still rude, increase the dosage of love! Love and kindness are the powerful magical weapons each one of us possesses and the trick is to use them the right way to win people's heart, make strong bonds and sustain relationships!"

Different people bring out different versions of you and you wouldn't have known that part of you existed until you meet that person.

Once my third girl went to full-time school, I wanted to do something for myself but didn't have a clear idea about my purpose. Every single day after dropping the girls at school, I would smile and wave at the other students. The simple act gave me boundless happiness but I didn't realize it was my calling! One fine day, I collected my art portfolio, my resume, and certificates and met my daughter's school principal, seeking a job. I was expecting a job as an art teacher but I was appointed as the English room teacher and also as a soft skill instructor.

1. The first best thing about all that happened was that the principal was able to look beyond my resume and knew where I could work better. She trusted me and my potential though I was a newcomer and hadn't had any experience as a teacher before.

2. The second best thing was that she allowed me to prepare my own course curriculum and lesson plan. I still remember the first lesson prepared for the students, "How to be happy?"

As I said before, people come in to your life when they have to, to show you your true potential and to push you to the next stage of your life. Grab the new opportunity and be aware of the change, do not fear.

Every morning at school, my day begins with doing my best to make as many students' day happier by just smiling, making eye contact while walking through the corridor, appreciating their neat hairdo, polished shoes, pressed uniform or smile.

The glow in the child's face actually makes my day too. It did make me feel elated and worthy. It takes a moment to make someone's day and one word to destroy someone's life. Your words have the power to hurt, heal, open minds, hearts and change the world. Be that change in this world. Never forget the responsibility you have over the words you speak. People who regularly help and uplift the mood of others are significantly happy and less likely to become depressed as they get older.

Sometimes you can't explain what you see in a person. It's just the way they take you to a place where no one else can. There can't be anything better than a good person with lots of love, care, affection, compassion, and empathy. You needn't be a celebrity to feel charismatic. Just caring for people and making them smile can make you the charismatic star!

People can change your whole day or can change your whole life sometimes. We meet people on purpose, either they have a role in our life or we have a role in theirs. God doesn't give you the people you want, instead he gives you the people you need to help you, hurt you, leave you, love you and make you the person you are meant to be. At the end of your life, you will never regret not having passed one more test, winning one more verdict or not closing one more deal. You will regret time not spent with your life partner, a parent, a friend or a child.

One of the best gifts you can give to someone is a genuine thank you for being in your life. I write handwritten letters and notes to people whom I love and cherish. People get drawn to you just by the way you make them feel.

Value relationships and grow them like how you water a sapling and raise it into a tree with stronger roots and branches.

Spend time and make any relationship work and grow until its roots spread deep inside in a way that in the long run the relationship and bond carry you in its arm during difficult days. I ask my daughters to be good friends to have many friends in their life. In the same way, relationships just don't happen... you need to grow, nurture and care for them.

Beauty is not just about having a pretty face. It's about having a pretty mind, a pretty heart, and a pretty soul. People grow when they are loved well. If you want to help others, heal and love them. An interesting moment happened at school when I started handling art classes too. The very first class was disturbed by two naughty boys who wouldn't sit or stop talking. I was unable to handle the class since they were bullying and picking fights with the other classmates. I realized they were deprived of attention and unconditional love. I called the students to the class front and made an announcement. "Class! I like them the most in this class just because they are energetic and interactive and so from now on they will sit next to me to attend the class." The boys were pretty shy and kept smiling while sitting beside me and in a couple of classes they were quite comfortable sitting next to me and they didn't disturb the class and the classmates ever. All that they wanted was plentiful appreciation and love. My mother-in-law Mrs. Roopavathi Johnson would always tell me one can be changed with love and affection. It really did work with the naughty boys!

Always leave people better than you found them - hug the hurt, kiss the broken, befriend the lost and love the lonely always because when you bring back the light in someone's life, the same light makes you feel warmer and look clearer.

I insist my girls and students to look out and make friends with the bully victims or the ones who are lonely and don't have company. Be the person who cares, who makes an effort and loves without hesitation. Be the person who makes people feel seen. Surround yourself with people that push you to do and be better. No drama or negativity. Just higher goals and higher motivation. Good times and positive energy. No jealousy or hate to bring out the absolute best in each other. Good people are like street lights along the roads. They don't make the distance short but they light up the path and make the walk easy and safe.

There is nothing stronger than someone who continues to stay soft in a world that hasn't always been kind to them. Be somebody who makes everyone feel like somebody. Leave everyone you meet better than you found them. Build someone up. Put their insecurities to sleep. Remind them that they are worthy. Tell them they are magical. Be the light in a too often dim world!

The world has a fair share of toxic and negative people. Insane people take a knife and stab people back but the wise ones use the knife to cut the cord and set themselves free from the insane toxic ones. When someone treats you like crap, remember it is because there is something wrong with them and not you. Normal people don't go around destroying other people's lives deliberately.

Learn to forgive a person who wasn't even sorry. That is your strength. Forgiveness makes you feel better and also helps you focus on much better things in your life. When you believe you are right, but still people criticize you, hurt you, shout at you - don't bother. Just remember… in every game, only the audiences make noises and not the players. Be a player, believe in yourself, and do your best!

Do not feel like a victim while sharing your story. You are indeed a survivor setting the world on fire with your truth. And you never know who needs your light, your warmth and courage. Do not let the behaviour of others destroy your inner peace. My mom Mrs. Vasanthakumari's advice for anyone would be, "Never let your inner self shiver when you speak to the person who hurt and tossed you in pain. Be bold to speak it out."

Be it any kind of relationship say friendship or marriage, love blooms and persists when the two persons are independent individuals. Love can flow only between two freedoms. Most marriages break when you try to control and dominate the other.

During a chat with my college mate and friend Mrs. Nithya Arvind, she shared her beautiful opinion. "The couples shouldn't ask for permission from the other to do anything or to go out and it shouldn't be last-minute information either. It should happen over a conversation, discussion, and opinion sharing always."

When it comes to raising your child, the life that you live in front of them speaks volumes and molds them on the right path. The way you talk, respect people, being a good host, how you handle your emotions like fear and anger, how hard you work, your fitness routine, how generous and helping you are, your smile, positivity and the way you keep people around happy matters a lot! Children learn everything by just looking at their parents and so make sure you are their perfect role model.

To raise a child who is comfortable enough to leave you means you have done your job incredibly. They are not ours to keep, our job is to teach them to soar on their own. A lifelong blessing for your children will be to fill them with warm memories of times together. Happy memories become a treasure in your child's heart to pull out on the future tough days.

People, relationships and bonds are temporary even with your family and children. Make sure you give them your best quality time and the most important thing is to see if your children or better half can survive in this world without you around. Training them to be on their own without your help is very important. Do not allow them to rely on you for everything. Allow them to deal with online payments, drawing cash from ATM, driving, cooking, bank transactions, paying rent, phone bills, taking care of children, taking care of themselves, etc. because people come into your life for a reason, a season or a lifetime. When you figure out which one it is, you will know what to do for each person. Never lose sight of the fact that the most important yardsticks of your success will be how you treat other people, your family, friends and co-workers, and even strangers you meet along the way.

People, bonding and relationship are magical and they are the best gift one can have - being blessed with people around, keeps your mind active and alive. Every person you meet on the journey has something to teach you... either good or bad. Learn the lesson and move on to the next stage of your life.

7. MENTAL HEALTH

Mental health is a state of well-being in which you realize your potential and can cope with the normal stresses of life, work productively and fruitfully and be able to make a contribution. It improves the quality of your life and when you are free of stress, worry and anxiety, you are more able to live your life to the fullest.

Mental health is equally important as our physical health, which most of us don't realize. Mental health strengthens and supports your ability to have healthy relationships, make good life choices, maintain physical health and wellbeing, handle the natural ups and downs of life to discover and grow towards your potential.

Mental health and physical health are fundamentally linked. There are multiple associations between mental health and physical conditions that significantly impact people's quality of life. Your body responds to the way you think, feel and act. This is often called the mind and body connection. When you are stressed, anxious or upset, your body tries to tell you that something is not right. High blood pressure or stomach ulcers might develop after a particularly stressful event such as the death of a loved one. Your body beautifully indicates when your emotional health is out of balance. Did you know that back pain, change in appetite, chest pain, dry mouth, constipation, diarrhea, extreme tiredness, aches, pains, headaches, palpitation, shortness of breath, stiff neck, sweating, weight gain or weight loss, and upset stomach are signs that your mental health needs immediate attention?

The cells in your body react to everything that your mind says. Negativity brings down your immune system. It is important to train your mind to see the good in every situation.

Food for your mind....

1. ***Think positively:*** I am blessed to stay positive in spite of any chaotic situation around me. When you look out for the positive side of any situation, your mind is calm and can work on solutions immediately.

A few days after we moved to our new home, Kandharaj and our pet dog Loki played fetch in the living room. The ball hit on the enormous killer whale painting that I had painted for hours together. I entered the room listening to the glass shattering and I could sense my husband was worried since it was one of my masterpieces. I was glad none were hurt and it was an opportunity to place a new painting. I handled the situation in a proactive manner. Instead if I had been a reactive wife, I am sure you would know the scenario of yelling, shouting, and argument.

Problem-solving: Problem-solving ability will work in full swing once you can stay positive. The base of the lake and the beautiful pebbles would be visible when the water is clear than when the lake is muddy. Keep your mind clear and calm in spite of the storm around. This can be achieved in the long process of living and learning the lessons. Spending time in nature, meditating regularly, committing random acts of kindness, keeping a daily gratitude journal and surrounding yourself with other positive people will let you stay positive and grounded.

2. ***Cherish the ones you love:*** School life and timetable comes to an end at one point but each day of mine is planned with a timetable and I do stick to it in spite of juggling my home, chores and girls. My time table would remind me to call a friend every Monday, visit my parents every Saturday, visit my bestie's mom every alternate Thursday, write handwritten letters, birthday notes or call

up to wish. I note down the birthday and anniversary dates of my loved ones to make their day.

Ultimately we are not going to carry with us any materialistic stuff when we leave this world, so make sure to carry loads of memories fastened to time well spent with your loved ones. A soul which detaches from the body and reaches heaven's gate, wouldn't be asked questions like,

- How many people did you like?

- How many friends did you have?

- How many people served food when you were their guest?

Instead you would be welcomed with questions like

- How many people liked you for the kindness and care you gave?

- How many called you their friend?

- How many people did you invite home and serve food?

If you don't have an answer to the above questions, well it is time to live the right way to get answers.

The living rooms wall in my previous home had these wordings hand painted by me,

My home will be a place where my family, friends, guests, and I find joy, comfort, peace, and happiness."

Reading through these lines, I was reminded about the simple commitments of life though they are the ones that bring happiness and are the stepping stone to reach the branches of life. Life is too short and you get old and your parents, aunt, uncle, and grandparents grow older too. You never realize it until you compare yourself or your parents to a candle that gives light to people around and melts every moment. Maybe one day the candle will be put off and our loved ones will leave us.

The darkness makes you realize and miss the warmth and light that the candle gave you when it was glowing. It is very difficult to see and regret the home where your parents lived, the things that they used and the place they once sat to relax expecting to spend more time with you. The pain is so miserable.

If you haven't spoken to your parents, siblings, friend or anybody, this is the right time to patch up and feel the love and cherish this awesome bond that you have been blessed in this birth. Make someone feel fabulous by giving a compliment, recording a playlist for them, sharing a hug, writing them a thoughtful card, treating them and being a listening ear.

3. ***Continue learning as long as you live:*** Learning doesn't stop with any particular age. It is a lifelong process and has a definite and specific impact on your brain. After you learn something new, your brain is never the same again. Important changes take place in your brain when you learn, which includes the creation of new connections between your neurons and making existing neural pathways stronger.

    Learning releases dopamine and is often exciting for the learner. Being in my early 40s, every single day can be spent on the couch, watching TV, napping, browsing, and just being lazy, eating and doing whatever I want to. But self-discipline is a must to keep one on track and I live by my small targets and goals which include reading a few pages from a book, online courses, workshops and also taking notes in my personal diary.

    Are you in your 50s, 60s, or 70s?

    Never mind. Just ask yourself what you wanted to learn during your childhood or is there something that you had always wanted to learn but didn't find time for yourself while juggling your family, home, and children? This is the time to become a student again and learn for yourself.

4. ***Learn from your mistakes:*** Nobody is perfect in this world though we work towards perfection. We commit a lot of mistakes from a very young age and learn the dos and don'ts. When an aged person advises us or stops us from doing certain acts, it means they have committed a similar mistake when they were young. The elderly people have the wisdom to guide us since they have learnt from their mistakes.

    The word EGO is the one that hinders your happiness by making you a stubborn hard nut who refuses to crack, in spite of knowing that you committed the mistake. Do not ask anyone around to judge you, judge yourself, and ask the voice of wisdom within you if you committed a mistake. Your conscience is your powerful weapon to rely upon. The first step is realization, the second step is acceptance, and the third step is 'change in behaviour'. Accepting and learning from your mistake, sharpens the happiness vibration.

5. ***Exercise daily to enhance your wellbeing:*** Daily simple workouts improves your mental health and self-esteem by reducing anxiety, depression, and negative mood. People who work out regularly have better mental health and emotional well-being and lower rates of mental illness. Exercise releases chemicals like endorphins and serotonin that improve your mood and sleep. Exercise pumps blood into the brain which makes you think more clearly. It increases the connections between the nerve cells in the brain. This improves your memory and helps protect your brain against injury and disease.

    I am a yoga person and I have been following the discipline of yoga routine every morning for the past 12 years. Missing my yoga routine makes me feel very guilty that I find time to squeeze in some asana in-between my meals or even before my bedtime. My day starts by 4:30 a.m. with Om chanting, 30 minutes of meditation, breathing exercises, neck and eye exercises, sun salutation (Suryanamaskaar), 35 asana and also face yoga.

6. ***Do not complicate your life unnecessarily:*** Life in a way is beautiful and the way we look at it is complicated. Issues keep coming up in life one after another to teach us a lesson or to grow from it so we become mature enough to step into the next stage of our life. Life is not cruel, it is a great teacher and once you learn to look at life from this paradigm, every day will be a miraculous and joyous beginning to try one more time.

Life is doing its best to evolve you into the person you are meant to be, to finish your task in this birth of yours. Its duty is to shake you, toss you, throw you down, make you wriggle in pain, cry, scream, and weaken you just to make you strong enough to leave a different person in the place you were. When life throws difficulties, don't run away, but instead face it, fight it, win it and learn the lesson to be learnt because it is your battle to fight and race to run.

Life has harsh ways of knocking you down and during times like that, do not ask "WHY ME?" but shout out tearing the sky "TRY ME!" with enormous courage and pride. Problems that might seem too big at this moment would be nothing in the next 5 years. When you turn back and review your past, you would feel crazy enough for worrying so much then.

7. ***Encourage and understand those around you:*** In this fast world everyone is super-fast to react, take revenge and make sure theirs is the last word or sentence in any argument or discussion. Learning to ask questions within you like,

"Is he having a bad day? Maybe her health is not good today! I know him, he is such a sweet and understanding person, and today if he is mad, then something must really be worrying him. Let me be patient."

These are signs that you are trying to understand the person and not being reactive and that you are proactive. Every person you meet is going through some difficulty that we never know, so let us encourage, appreciate and understand people during this short time we live together as a family, team, or class. Once you are aware of the power of encouragement and appreciation, it would be the easiest weapon to win, make new friendships, stronger bonds and complete never-ending tasks.

My little girl Inicka once told me that she used to love the way I keep my room with pleasant color theme sheets and matching cushion covers on my bay window. I turned back and noticed that the sheets and covers didn't match and they were lazy colors. That spark in her appreciation got in me instantly and the whole week I took pains to keep the home, tried out new arrangements, maintained smooth and wrinkle free bed spreads and also potted some indoor plants for an aesthetic look. I did thank Inicka for bringing back the magic in me and encouraged her to appreciate more people in the future particularly people who need more appreciation to do more and to feel valued.

8. ***Do not give up:*** The present generations are so sensitive, and timid, and give up very easily. Life will not be a bed of roses always. Life can be compared to a flowing river and the two banks are happiness on one end and sorrow on the other. Life rubs through both the banks and we don't have a choice.

   A boxing match is the best game to be compared, to learn about life and not give up anytime. Life will shower its hard blows on you. You will be beaten up and floored. You wouldn't have the stamina to get back. You don't lose when you fall but you lose when you refuse to get up. It is like the same way the floored boxer is given 10 seconds to get up… take your time to dust yourself, shed a tear, and get back on your feet to fight again. You are out of the game when you give up or fail to get up. Remember! It is your game and battle, if it is not you, who else would fight?

20 years back I was not the same person who I am today. I was timid, a coward to fight life, rolled through good and bad times and also felt like I couldn't pull myself out of the struggle and misery and felt lost in the rough ocean. And I am ever grateful to the tough times in my life which gave me wisdom to guide people, to handle counselling sessions, to become a speaker, happiness and life coach and last but not the least to make me an author of this book! It is truly amazing to look at the way life molds you. Like how any gold ore goes through a tough process of melting and hammering to become an expensive jewelry, life gives pain to model us as one valuable masterpiece. Unfortunately people become losers, unable to bear the pain and quit in-between. Your day is much closer… until then hold on tight to the reigns of your life and keep riding further.

9. ***Discover and nurture your talents:*** Every child born in this world has an inborn talent that is hidden deep inside. There can't be one person who is born talentless. The first person to identify your talent is your mom and the second person to find your talent is your second mom, your teacher. In the worst case, if you couldn't find your talent, you can question yourself,

"What activity is it that I love doing with my heart and soul, for hours together, without losing my energy and feel like doing more and don't feel the need to stop?"

That is your talent and potential! If you can make your talent, hobby, or passion a source of your income, you wouldn't feel the work stress at any point in time and money flows in abundance. Let me introduce you to a new term "Sharpening the saw". Whatever skill or talent that you may possess needs to be fine-tuned or sharpened by learning more about it through books, browsing, online courses, or even classes from tutors. I knew my talent was art and though I was a self-taught artist, I took classes from various tutors to sharpen my art skill and gain exposure to various techniques and mediums. It is simple, you need to keep yourself updated to keep flowing in the main stream.

THE THINGS YOU ARE PASSIONATE ABOUT ARE NOT RANDOM, THEY ARE YOUR CALLING!

10. *Set goals for yourself*: Athletes who begin from a very young age achieve at school level, state level, national level, and finally international level. Once they reach the peak, most of the athletes don't have next level target and feel blank and depressed. Likewise, when we don't have any goals and targets, life becomes lethargic and gloomy and you tend to become unproductive.

As a homemaker I have few targets. As a bookworm, I do have a goal to finish the book in a week or two. I fix a target to read 20 pages every day. Accomplishing small goals will instantly make you feel happy and valued. Your self-confidence level shoots up and have the urge to be more productive and achieve more.

Here is a sample of a target chart to clean a home:

Table 1

MONDAY	TUESDAY	WEDNESDAY
BEDROOM DAY Change sheets Sweep/Vacuum floors Declutter 10 min	**BATHROOM DAY** Clean shower and toilet clean sink, counter sweep &mop floors clean mirror	**KITCHEN DAY** clean out refrigerator clean counters clean table and chairs sweep and mop floors
THURSDAY	**FRIDAY**	**SATURDAY**
LIVING ROOM DAY dust & polish furniture clean tv freshen fabrics sweep/vacuum floors	**ALTERNATE** week 1- all appliances week 2- kitchen cabinets week 3- windows &blinds week 4- walls and baseboards	**OUTSIDE** clean out car garage and garden cleaning sweep off steps yard work

The goals may be big or small, but they are the best vehicles to keep you inspired as you walk through your life. When you try to reach your goals, the desire to reach the destination will pull you through the tough times.

If you are a mentally strong person, you will enjoy your time alone, take responsibility for your actions, live in the present by being mindful, will be able to focus on the tasks at hand, embrace, celebrate change and have great health habits and own your mind, body, and spirit, celebrate the success of others and surround yourself with greatness. Set goals to keep yourself busy and happier.

8. RULE AND TRAIN YOUR MIND

It is very important to train your mind as early as possible to remain calm even during trying situations to think clearly and solve issues. Did you know your mind is shaped by the books you read? Book reading disciplines your mind and whatever you read, you are exposing your mind to new thoughts and ideas that you can brood and practice in your life. Analyze what types of books you might love reading. I have my library filled with motivational, inspirational books, books on psychology and mind, Buddha's teachings and meditation techniques, books written by Buddhist monks and history of places and temples.

The person you will be in five years depends largely on the information you feed your mind today. I am very particular about with whom I interact and what I expose my mind to – be it books, tv shows, or movies. I never read newspapers or watch any news channels. Likewise, I space myself from people who gossip, complain, are jealous, possessive, and negative. These people can easily suck the positive vibes from me and make me feel weak and drained out.

My first experience of being with a negative person was during the first year of my college. The girl I got introduced at class was possessive to the core that she wouldn't let me interact with others. Fights and arguments would be staged when I interact with other classmates and nothing that I did for her would please her. It went to an extent where I would sob after college hours not knowing a way to please her and unable to know where I went wrong.

During the second year of college, she dropped out and her presence and absence made such a vast difference. I was way too happier, more cheerful and interactive. Sometimes it does take time to realize we are amidst toxic people and that we can't please them and there is no need to please them by sacrificing your happiness.

Books like Secret by Rhonda Byrne and The power of the subconscious mind by Joseph Murphy can discipline your mind and can make you realize the power of positive thoughts to use your mind and draw luck perfectly into your life. The exact way to train your mind is how the ring master trains a lion. Like how the whip makes the lion listen to the master, awareness and mindfulness make your mind listen to you. You are the master and your mind should always be the slave, but once you start listening to your mind and act as your mind says, you become the slave and the mind becomes the master.

Well, what happens when you are the slave of your mind? You fall prey to it. Procrastination sets in. You become lazy, don't have the urge to try new ideas, postpone duties, believe you still have more time and in the worst case people become addicted to games, gadgets, social media, alcohol, smoking or even drugs. Disciplining your mind comes first. The instant one negative thought crosses your mind, you need to check on it. The mind has the funny habit of focusing on what you don't want or try to avoid and forget. Your job is to train it so it can focus on what you want.

Negative thoughts creep in very easily and that is purely natural. What should you do to stop or curb negative thoughts? Practice replacing your thought with a new positive one. How do you do it?

Let me explain this with a simple example. When you get in your vehicle to start on any long journey, it is quite natural for your mind to think if you would reach safe or what would happen when you meet a road accident and no wonder your thoughts are interconnected that you get totally spaced out thinking about what would happen to your family and your mind would be replaying the last ceremonial rites!

The best part about training your mind is an awareness that you are thinking about the unwanted.

How can you replace your thoughts?

Come back to the present moment and be mindful of what is happening around you. Overlap the negative thought with a positive one by visualizing your safe journey and seeing yourself reaching your destination or your family and also imagining your pets and children greeting you with enthusiasm. Complete the visualization with gratitude,

"I am happy and grateful for my perfect and safe journey.

Thank you! Thank you! Thank you!"

Every time you practice this replacement of thoughts you are rewiring your brain and at one point your brain processes only positive thoughts. This method has been helpful over the years to master my mind and the occurrence of negative thought has reduced drastically.

Robin Sharma puts the whole thing of training your mind beautifully. He compares your mind to a beautiful garden and you are the gardener. When you allow one weed (negative thought) to grow and take its form, the small weed grows and takes over the whole garden in no time ransacking the whole garden (mind). The weed might seem to be so trivial but in no time it can take a life of its own, grow huge and massive by suppressing your mind and the positivity of your garden. The gardener's (your) job is to be watchful and not allow even one negative weed no matter how small it may be.

Flush the unwanted negative thoughts from your mind thrice a day and the best time is when you sit for your meal. Close your eyes and imagine a suction pump that descends from above and imagine the heavy negative thoughts getting sucked out of your mind.

The lesser the traffic of thoughts in your mind, the easier the journey of life!

9. SELF LOVE

The relationship with yourself sets the tone for every other relationship you have.

My favourite person in this whole world and the person I love the most is ME! I have always cared for myself more than anyone and that might sound so selfish but that is completely okay. You need to fall in love with the way you really are… your skin tone, complexion, the texture of your hair, the birthmarks on your skin, your voice, your potential, talent and lot more! When you can't appreciate and love yourself, how can you expect others to love you? Feel comfortable in your own body and enjoy the person as who you have been created just for a purpose and there is no one exactly like you in this whole world!! Instead of wishing you were someone else, be proud of who you are because you never know who was looking at you wishing they were you.

Be kind to yourself, and respect your body by taking good care of your vehicle (body) given for this whole lifetime. Practice workouts, meditation, breathing exercises and pamper your body with enough sleep and rest. The way you care for your body now will give you more longevity and also a healthy body where you needn't depend on anyone until the moment of your death. Being bedridden, immobile and becoming a burden to your children and family is very painful. If you haven't given a thought to this, it is time to start with your exercise routine NOW.

In spite of the busy schedule, I take time to go for a head massage and just sink and relax on the spa's chair forgetting about my routine and pending chores. Truly that is heaven! And it is quite okay to try new hair do's, new costumes, visit places alone, read a book for hours, sing madly and dance as if you are a pro.

The best thing I did once for myself was during one period of my time when I really needed a break from my tight schedule.

My friends weren't available for a call either and I did try waiting for a couple of days and lost patience for someone to check on me or pamper me. That noon after my classes at school were over, I took myself to a café, ordered my favourite food, picked a book and settled down for nearly an hour and a half reading my favourite book in a new environment. Yes! I took myself out :)

Sometimes when the whole world is unavailable, all that you have got is YOU. You are there for yourself, to pamper yourself and make you fall in love all over again. And to do that you need to know more about yourself. Your likes, dislikes, passion and everything about you should be at your fingertips. My dream journal session with students has one topic called 'My instant happiness'. It is all about what makes you happy immediately to get recharged in a moment.

I have also been practicing journaling to monitor my thoughts and emotions. Journaling and self-love are connected in a way to reduce anxiety, depression and mental health problems. You get to know yourself better, provide a sense of clarity, build self-worth, help you organize and analyze problems, put things into perspective and improve your relationship with others.

This is one beautiful story that I narrate to my class often to make them understand the need for self-love and quality time for themselves:

There was a man who was cheerful and would brim with happiness, positivity and socialize with everyone at work. He never committed to joining anyone on all Sundays in spite of the pressure from his colleagues to eat out or to watch movies. He always refused the invites since he had the priority to meet an important person on Sundays. The meeting with that important person every Sunday makes him himself and is the secret behind his success, positivity, happy and cheerful self. This made his friends and colleagues so curious and they wanted to meet this very important person at least once. The following Sunday, everyone visited his home without prior information. Looking at the uninvited guests, he was surprised and shocked as well. The colleagues were stubborn to meet the important person and so finally the man revealed that it was none other than him.

Nobody could believe him and still wondered what is happening?!

After the whole week of busy schedule, he spends time at home with himself doing art, exercise, yoga, meditation, watching movies, listening to music, gardening, cooking, sleeping, relaxing, watching sunsets and sunrise and did whatever that his soul needed to recharge for the upcoming week. He also added that he loves pampering himself and he deserves that at all times because it is he who has to take care of his mental and physical health. Liking yourself and quality ME time brings about more energy, happiness, productivity, creativity and whatever you want from inside you.

The answers you seek never come when the mind is busy, they come when the mind is still. Take some time alone every now and then to meet that amazing person inside you. Love yourself! It is important to stay positive because beauty comes from the inside out. When you love yourself, you glow from the inside by attracting people who love, respect and appreciate your energy. Everything starts with you and how you feel about yourself!

Remember to be yourself and to embrace your funny humorous self, your inner child particularly. Some will love the way you are, whereas others won't! But who cares? Worry about loving yourself, instead of loving the idea of other people loving you. Self-love is so important because when you find yourself crying on the bathroom floor, who is going to be there for you? YOU. You have to pick yourself up and find the strength to move on. At the end of the day, you are all you have got. We came alone and will be leaving alone. Taking care of yourself is your prior responsibility.

10. SELF ESTEEM

What is self-esteem?

It is a term that explains a person's sense of personal worth and value. It is all about how much you appreciate and like yourself in spite of the circumstances. Having healthy self-esteem can influence your motivation, your mental well-being and your overall quality of life. However having self-esteem that is either too high or too low can be problematic. Striking a balance here is important. In simple words, self-esteem is our belief about ourselves. How capable and loved do we feel?! It is our shield against life's challenges.

Unfortunately, self-esteem is a self-fulfilling prophecy. The worse you feel about who you are and what you do, the less motivated you will be to build your self-esteem. From here you easily spiral down into a cycle of negative thinking by keeping yourself tangled in damaging false beliefs.

Causes of low self-esteem:

Your self-esteem level can dwindle due to stressful life events such as relationship breakdown, financial trouble, poor treatment from a partner, parent or career, or even being in an abusive relationship. Ongoing medical problems such as chronic pain, serious illness or physical disability can also play with your self-esteem level. Say a stubborn "No" when you have to change yourself to please the people around you because that is exactly where your self-esteem level dips.

If your self-esteem level is still low, sit in a calm place and continue reading the topic...

If you don't design your life plan, chances are you will fall into someone else's plan. And guess what they have planned for you? Not much. One small crack doesn't mean you are broken. It means that you were tested and you didn't fall apart.

Worrying is a waste of time. Good and bad things happen in your life, you just have to keep living and not stress over what you can't control. Feelings and emotions are like the sea waves that rub on your feet. Well, you cannot stop them from coming, but you can decide which ones to give life to. Appreciate where you are in your journey even if it is not where you want to be. Every season serves a purpose. And seasons do change. They are not permanent. So are your pain and sufferings in life. Do not let the behavior of others destroy your inner peace.

Start feeling worthy, valuable, and deserving of receiving the best that life has to offer. Be magnetic!

You can't go back and change the beginning, but you can start where you are and change the ending. You will continue to suffer if you have an emotional reaction to everything that is said to you. True power is sitting back and observing things with logic. True power is restraint. If words control you, it means everyone else can control you. Breathe and allow things to pass. A house built with straw gets blown away more easily during a storm than a house built with cement and brick. It stands undisturbed by the harsh storm blowing. You should know how vital it is to build yourself stronger from deep inside in such a way that you are stable at all times in spite of the chaos and the chaotic people around you.

Whenever you find yourself doubting how far you can go, just remember how far you have come:

- Remember everything you have faced, all the battles you have won and all the fears you have overcome.

- Respect yourself enough to walk away from anything that no longer makes you happy.

- Accept both compliments and criticism, it takes both sun and rain for a flower to grow.

- When everything seems to be going wrong, it means old energy is clearing out for new energy to enter.

- Be patient and trust the good things coming.

Sometimes God closes doors because it is time to move forward. He knows you won't move unless your circumstances force you. Trust the transition God has got for you. You must be willing to get rid of the life you have planned, so as to have the life that is waiting for you. When a door closes, knock on it a few times. But if it still doesn't open, let it stay closed. In your career, in love, in life, when you see the full stop at the end of a sentence, don't try and turn it on to a comma. Know when something is over and move on.

You have this one life. How do you want to spend it? Apologizing? Regretting? Questioning? Hating yourself? Dieting? Running after people who don't see you?

Be brave. Believe in yourself. Do what feels good. Take risks. You have this one life. Make yourself proud. It is never late to ask yourself,

__"Am I ready to change my life? Am I ready to change myself?"__

However old you are, whatever you went through, it is always possible to be reborn. Every breath is a chance to be reborn.

When you write the story of your life, do not let anyone else hold the pen!

<u>Ways to lift your self-esteem level:</u>

It is important to check on the level of your self-esteem bucket and also to fill in your self-esteem bucket:

• Surround yourself with people that push you to do and be better. No drama or negativity. Just higher goals and motivation. Good times and positive energy. No jealousy or hate. Simply bringing out the positive best in each other.

- Everything you do to raise the self-esteem of others raises your own self-esteem at the same time.   Build someone up. Put their insecurities to sleep. Remind them they are worthy. Tell them they are magical. Be a light in a too often dim world. Be there for someone who needs your guidance, your leadership, and your support.

  Watching them progress with your help will add to your self-esteem and self-respect. Let negative people go. If there are negative people in your life who have nothing positive to say or who put you down or took advantage of you, let them go. The only way to find your self-esteem is to surround yourself with supportive positive people who admire and value you.

- Never underestimate the healing power of listening to your favorite music on full blast while jumping around the home like an idiot.

- Keeping your home clean can help you increase your self-esteem too.

- Do something creative. Creativity stimulates the brain. Pull out your old guitar, write a story or poem and take a dance class.

- Read something inspirational. A great way to gain more self-esteem is to read something that lifts you and makes you feel positive about yourself.

- Love your life. Take pictures of everything. Tell people you love them. Talk to random strangers.

- Do things you are scared to do. Stand at the edge of your comfort zone. Stretch yourself and move to the edge of your comfort zone. Get uncomfortable by trying something new and meet different people. Confidence begins at the edge of your comfort zone.

- Take your life and make it the best story in the world. Help someone, use your talent, skill and ability to help others. Give someone direct assistance, share helpful resources or teach someone something they want to learn. Offer something you do well as a gift to someone.

- Stop worrying about what others think because when you do, you never feel free to be completely yourself. Make a firm decision to stop worrying about what other people think and begin making choices based on what you want and not what you think others want from you.

- Believe in yourself and gather the courage. Heal your past. Unresolved issues and drama can keep you trapped in low self-esteem. Seek the support of a counselor to help you heal the past so you can move on to the future in a confident and self-assured way.

- The best way to find your self-esteem is to create personal boundaries. Know what your boundaries are and how you wish to respond when people cross them. Don't allow others to control you, take advantage of you or manipulate you. To be confident is to maintain firm boundaries.

- Care about your appearance. When you look your best, you feel your best. Dress like someone who has confidence and let your self-assurance come through in how you look. It is always a must to wake up, follow the routine of workout, meditation, dress up and get out of the house.

- Welcome failure as part of your growth. It is a common response to be hard on yourself when you have failed. But if you can shift your thinking to understand that failure is an opportunity to learn and grow, it can help you.

- Always remain a student. Think of yourself as a lifelong learner. Approach everything that you do with a student's mentality. Zen Buddhists call it a beginner's mind - open, eager, unbiased and willing to learn.

- Face your fear. Allow yourself to feel afraid but keep going anyway. Self-esteem is often found in the dance between your deepest desires and your greatest fears.

- Be optimistic and treat yourself well. Challenge your limiting beliefs. When you catch yourself thinking negative about yourself, stop and challenge yourself. Don't let yourself be limited by false beliefs.

- Participate in life and know the purpose of your life and birth. Determine what your values are and examine your life to see where you are not living in alignment with what you believe and make necessary changes.

11. GIVERS ARE GETTERS

Rev Dr. Bhikku Bodhipala says the best way to earn good karma is by learning to give and serve the needy. We have taken so many births as birds, animals, insects and crawling creatures in our previous lifetimes to finally take this human birth. If you had known how many births you had taken before and suffered, you wouldn't waste a second of this human birth and also plan this life perfectly and live each day with gratitude. I advise my students to give once they get when they grow and earn for themselves. It is a must to learn the habit of service and giving to not only earn good karma but also to have a better next birth and to make the income stay and multiply forever.

The law works this way:

When a person gives away 10% of his salary or monthly income as donation or charity for food or education, the person's income miraculously multiplies and keeps multiplying as long as he keeps giving the 10% from his earnings every month.

Right from childhood, encourage your children to practice giving, so it becomes a habit and sticks to them like a second skin. Children and adults who give are happier, self-less, self-contained, easy-going, have a positive outlook towards life, compassionate, empathetic, loving, caring and learn to keep people around them happier. The moment your children see that you are a giver by visiting old age homes, orphanages and helping some random stranger in the street, they follow your footsteps obviously. Once they feel the joy of giving, they will crave for more of this kind of happiness.

Explaining about givers are getters to my children, it did have a miraculous result when my second girl Ela was in her 2nd grade. That evening before picking her back from school, I visited a stationary shop to get some art supplies for myself and happened to run into a new brand of glue and got 3 pieces of glue pen. On the way back home from school, I handed over the 3 glue pens to her and she was surprised to get them and told me what had happened that day. One of her classmates ran out of glue and asked if Ela was willing to share. Ela remembered the law of giving and getting. So, she kept a portion for herself and squeezed the entire glue into her classmate's glue bottle. She was delighted since she got 3 new glue's within a few hours of giving them. Not sure if Ela knew how surprised and proud I felt that day!

It is a normal thought to cross your mind when you see someone getting paid more than you and accumulate profit easily when you work hard for a monthly salary. Also, they have a gigantic house, car and latest gadgets. This feeling is misunderstood by many as jealousy. It is not that! It can be labeled as craving, a burning YES, hunger, thirst, desire, wish, want and dream. The thought is quite unavoidable but it is a must to handle it because your mind has the potential to cook these thoughts into true jealousy that if you allow it to take over, there are chances of you losing what you already have like money, property, job and even people.

I chant an affirmation in my mind with my heart and soul to bless the person and situation so they are blessed with more and more of what they have. Don't you think that is the best way of being a human to bless him with more luck and success in life?

<u>Make it a practice to repeat this affirmation when you feel a craving the next time:</u>

"I wish for their abundance in wealth. I rejoice in his prosperity. May he be blessed with more and more."

Remember to give more if you want more and this blessing of human life is quite rare and a boon to confirm you are a human!!

12. SURROUND YOURSELF WITH HAPPY PEOPLE

The importance of happy people are known when we have trying situations and stormy days. Happy people act like a charging station when we are depleted of energy. The power and energy manifested by happy people are so huge that it is contagious. When you spend a few minutes with these kinds of people you will be revived easily by their pure aura. You might have had a very difficult day at work… Remember to make a call or visit the person whom you think can wash out the negative energy and mindset from you instantly.

The moment you realize your battery is going to drain out, it is much more advantageous in a way to prevent getting into loneliness and depression. Happy people are like game changers and in no time you will spring back with energy and be your own self.

It is time to earn such happy people in your life to stay on track and hold on to the reigns of life. Happy people can be your life partner, friend, bestie, parents, siblings, colleagues and even your kids or pets. Never allow them to slip off from your life because you need them more than they need you.

Happy people share a bit of their positive mindset with you to make you happy, embrace your pain, give comfort, boost your self-esteem level, give a strong support, safeguard your mind from negative triggers, they can bring you up, help you remind your dreams and to chase them. They are the ones who can crack the immense problem to pieces and make you deal with one part at a time and also remind you never to sweat the small stuff.

The best lesson a happy person can teach you is to smile again when you have forgotten to smile and to live life in the present moment. Before searching for a happy person, it is time you become one to keep the many others around you happy too. Making others happy, multiplies your happiness!

The energy emitted by a happy person is like a cloud of magical dust that can fill the room the person is in. For instance, an upset person enters the room after a bad day. He does not have any interaction with the happy person but the moment he enters the room, he feels light, happy and ideas pop in, to solve the issue, becomes creative or the issue looks so small at the moment. Questions run through his mind, unable to understand what happened to them all on a sudden to feel different and refreshed. Staying in the company of a happy person is magical. It is a blessing always when people voice when they feel so happy and positive after they meet me or just visit my home :)

<u>13. KNOWING YOUR PURPOSE IN LIFE</u>

Knowing the purpose in your life or the reason for your birth is vital because people who know the purpose of their birth are happier carrying out their destined part. But how do you know your purpose in life? The purpose of life is always tangled with the talent or potential you are born with.

As God created human beings, he packed each one of us with a skill or individual potential. There can't be even one child who was sent to this world without a talent bestowed upon them. It is already in there and it is the role of the parent or teacher to find the individuality. Sometimes when it is not known, the talent in you will shine like the streak of morning sunlight through the clouds one fine day when it is time to reveal the inborn talent hidden in you.

A few inquisitive students would ask if there is any other way to immediately know their capability. Their tiny little faces would bloom when I say yes. If you have enjoyed doing a few works from your heart and soul you would have worked for hours together but would have not been tired a bit and still have the craving to do more of it. That is your talent or what you are good at. This is your passion as it never tires you or takes away your interest.

What are you supposed to do after finding your talent? The next step is to sharpen the talent so it can be put to use effectively. The talent in you could be your voice, art, music, dance, writing, reading, sports or anything. Sharpening your talent means taking extra classes from tutors who can bring out your full potential and make you shine like a star in your field.

Apart from the talent and life you have, you are to live with it. Each one of our purpose in life is to be happy and enjoy every moment and the journey of life. The purpose of one's life might be very simple or complicated according to destiny.

Once I discovered my purpose in life, I have been living my life to the fullest and I should say I am much happier than before. I compare myself to a flower that blooms in the morning and droops the same evening having a way too short life. Though the flower's life is just for a few hours it does its duty to the utmost by attracting passers-by, spreading its unique fragrance, making one stop by, admire and smile at it and making the people around happy. Though the flower knows its life span is short, it doesn't worry about it, it lives in the moment facing rainy and sunny days with its head held high.

My purpose in life is to be happy and keep the people around me happy too, to show people the light during their dark days and merge them back with life's flow when they are out of track. When you know your life's purpose, you gain a meaning to live and every single day is a gift not to be wasted worrying about people who hurt you, left you stranded, put you in a difficult situation, insulted you, cheated you, and made you struggle.

Look deeper into your life to seek the purpose that is waiting for you and only you. It is your destined job and none other than you is qualified enough to finish it on time. Time is ticking by buddy. Never waste a moment of your life and make this life of yours a valuable and worthy one. We are given the best birth to realize the purpose of each one's life and fulfill it. The things you are passionate about are not random, they are your calling. Listen to your call closely to be there and do it before it is time.

14. STARTING YOUR DAY WITH A SMILE

A day goes good or bad depending on your thoughts and how you start your day. Your whole day depends on you. Starting the day with a smile or a forceful smile keeps your vibes high and things can't bring you down that easily. A smile should be made an inseparable part of your outfit and remember to wear one when you do everything and communicate with people.

A smile is one's personal weapon and power to handle and fight out anything bothering you. Sometimes having a smile on your face doesn't come naturally. Smiling because you must and not because you want to does make a difference.

Keeping a happy thought in the back of your mind brings about a natural smile from your heart and soul. Taking some time out of your day and thinking of some moments in your life that made you happy will make you talk overjoyed. It is helpful to have some happy thoughts in your bank, for when you need some extra help to get a genuine smile.

Smiling helps you stay positive and that is a good reason why you should start your day with a smile and continue that smile throughout the day. The kind of thoughts you think of, right when you wake up in the morning can set the tone of how your day is going to go. You would have heard of the phrase,

"He woke up on the wrong side of the bed this morning."

When the first thought of the day is not a good one, the chances of you being cranky or in a foul mood the whole day are high. You and only you decide on how your day is going to go. Do not let anyone or anything bring you down and wipe the smile off your face.

Look into the mirror every day after you wake up and give a genuine smile to yourself and you deserve that. Observe the skin tone, messy hair, puffed-up eyes, sleepy face, and the smile. That is the best way to start your day!

These could help you start your day with a smile:

1. <u>Start your day with an affirmation or mantra:</u>

When the sun rises, rise along and tell yourself it is going to be a great day. Demand yourself to have a great day. You may even write it down and hang it up on your wall, so you will be able to see it right when you wake up. The affirmation can be simple as,

"Today is going to be great. I am going to seize the day and be happy because I DESERVE IT."

The affirmation fulfills the purpose of reminding you to focus on the good side of life because you deserve to be happy.

2. <u>Think happy thoughts:</u>

Thinking happy thoughts does so much for your brain and your health. Positive thoughts decrease cortisol and produce serotonin, which generates a perception of well-being. This also helps your brain function at peak capacity.

3. <u>Be thankful:</u>

Do you have a house?

Do you own a car?

Have you got food on the table?

Are there clean clothes and towels every day?

These are things to be thankful for. You don't have to have some experience or item to be grateful for. You will have to focus on what you already have and know that you are truly blessed and be thankful for that. Being grateful for everything that you have is one of the best ways to provoke a smile on your face.

The more we continue to smile and keep smiling, the better we will feel and it won't take long to notice a difference in our attitude. No wonder smile is a curve that sets so many relationships straight.

Enjoy some quiet time before you rush into the world each morning. Spend time with a pet, fluff a pillow, read a poem, water a plant and watch the steam rise from your coffee. All of this chosen peace will serve as a powerful prayer for more peace. It will represent your request to the universe for calmness and clarity in your day.

15. STRESS AND ANXIETY

The stress and anxiety that you experience are caused by the reaction to the people or the situation. Stress builds when you don't plan your work or day well ahead. Every time when I have to get ready and leave home early the next morning, I would pack my bag the day before so I don't miss anything and also don't have the stress of last-minute packing. My dressing table will have the clothes that I plan to wear for the next day along with the accessories. Taking a shower before bed is one best ways to keep away stress. You are eventually creating more time for the next day and the important thing to note is that last-minute stress is avoided.

Function and celebration days were tougher for 4 ladies in my house to get dressed and leave home on time. So, my girls and I choose the clothes needed the previous day for a less chaotic day.

My food menu for the following week is planned every Sunday to avoid breaking my head to decide on the menu. This is one more difficult task for a woman to plan for the menu each day than cooking a complete meal.

Planning is the key to avoiding stress anytime and even new mothers can plan for a day out with their baby by packing the bag the day before with extra clothes, diapers, wet wipes, sterilized bottles, and getting armed the previous night for a peaceful battle.

I had the habit of carrying a set of different toys and books in the baby bag so they don't get bored easily with the new stuff that they are exposed to. I never pick toys from the toy box at home. Carrying containers with colorful foods like boiled carrot sticks and peas was so handy with my girls. While at the restaurant, the food on their high chair keeps their mouth and hands occupied because they handpick each food slowly.

Working as a teacher, planning helped me to keep stress completely away because I have my lesson plan done for the whole year and also collect the related images and videos for the class every Sunday. I plan, teach and train the students for any upcoming art competitions by practicing the artwork once myself and I get a color copy of the artwork for the student. I sit beside the student and guide them to draw, shade and add finishing touches for a couple of days.

Every single day before the competition, the time is allotted and the student is encouraged to complete the artwork with perfection on time. Repetition of the same art within the time allotted builds perfection and confidence in the student. A day before the competition, an envisioning exercise is practiced with the student. They envision the competition day, seated in the venue, working on the art in a grounded and peaceful manner, and at last carrying the trophy back to school through their mind's eye. No wonder this planning has always bagged prizes and trophies for the students. Planning is the key!

I learned planning from my mother. I have seen her plan for big days like marriages without any stress. She would bring all that is needed for the big day to the specific room. The stuff would be packed in individual bags. The bag will be loaded into the car on the big day and nothing would be forgotten or left behind.

Every single thing needs planning. I usually pull a long face when I have to clear the dining and kitchen counter after dinner, to sort the vessels, wash them and clean the counters. Playing my favorite music track speeds up the work and it is also fun dancing along and humming as the work gets completed. I also load the dishwasher and laundry machine the previous night with clothes and the detergent compartment filled in. The next morning all that I do is turn it on like a power queen ;)

Procrastination and postponing the day's work is the major cause of stress at home or in office. Be energetic enough to do the work right away. You can avoid the big-time work of arranging and rearranging the home or workplace by at once clearing the space that you used or worked.

Before I leave a room, I turn back to take a glance to pick up any used vessels, glasses or t.v remotes. I align the furniture and cushions in place and trash tissues or paper bits lying down. It saves much of your precious time when you take a look to set things in order before leaving a room.

My girls as toddlers would leave their toys scattered after playtime. I never allowed them to pick more than one box at a time and once they are done playing, we have the cleanup session. We pick and drop into the box and then get the next box. I was able to instill good habits and responsibility as they were growing up.

Coming up to the workers' payday, I was at ease calculating the salary, leave days, and the money got in advance because as and when they take leave or get advance, I note down the date and reason for the leave taken and money got. This has avoided issues so many times when the maidens or workers forget. Stress is created by us always and not by the people or the surrounding.

Unhandled stress leads the way to the next stage called anxiety. Anxiety is your body's natural response to stress. It is a feeling of fear about what is to come. On the first day of school, a job interview, or giving a speech may cause people to feel fearful and nervous.

Don't believe in your thought of every single eye looking at you and observing your moves. People around have their own work to do and keep moving. When you visit a new place, plan it in your mind where are you going to sit, is there anyone smiling at you? Smile back. If u have any known faces, walk to them and find a seat beside them.

It is only your mind shooting up so many questions to create anxiety. Never fail to remind your mind that it is your slave and you are the master. Facing the situation this way helps handle situations in a better way and you come to better terms with yourself.

Get healthy habits of getting enough sleep, meditating, staying active, exercising, eating a healthy diet, avoiding alcohol, avoiding caffeine and quitting smoking. Keep a thorough check on your daily routine and job to keep away stress and anxiety completely.

Also check your mind if it is dwelling in the present, past or future. A mind that dwells in the past will have stress and the mind which dwells in the future will have anxiety for sure. Happy people are the ones who are mindful of the present and take one day at a time and live it to the fullest.

Be wise! Complaining about the past and not being able to forgive people will ruin your present and also your future. Plan for the future but do not get anxious about it. Stay positive and hope for a better future because stress degenerates your body cells and can minimize your longevity.

16. HARD TIMES, PAIN, PROBLEM, AND SUFFERING

During sulky sad days, always remember:

Pain is part of growing and everything in life is temporary.

Complaining and worrying changes nothing. Your scars are symbols of your strength. Other people's negativity is not your problem and every little struggle is not your problem. What is meant to be will eventually BE. The best thing you can do is stay calm, wait for the storm to pass and keep going.

Life has its own way of settling us back when we don't expect it or deserve it. It is most likely to happen when we are at the top of our game that our greatest suffering begins. All that is dear to us can be taken away, leaving us sitting in the darkness and facing the depth. It is in those times of greatest pain that our true character is revealed and we are introduced to our finest strengths.

Failure and suffering are our best friends in life. When one door closes, another opens. But we often look so long with regret upon the closed door that we fail to see the one that is opened for us. Our wounds and pain give us wisdom. The days you fall will become your stepping stones to the next stage of your life. Pain leads you to your strength always.

Hard times are often blessings in disguise that we fail to realize. Allow life to strengthen you. Learn to keep your head high and keep going no matter how badly it hurts. Everyone has a rough day, a bad month, and a crappy year. Sometimes the hardest lessons to learn are the ones your spirits need the most. Your past can never be a mistake when you have well-read the lesson from it. The experiences you had so far need to be put in a box labeled "Thank You"!

When it is time to make a change, the universe makes it so uncomfortable for you that you will have no choice but to leave. When you are not happy in a situation, don't stay in denial and try to make it work. The world has better plans for you. Trust in the process and do your part by aligning yourself with the things you want. You will face a lot of people to get you there to the place you are meant to be. It takes hurt, pain, healing, rejection, redirection, loss, battle and resiliency to grow.

You must remember how much you have survived and your world has fallen apart. The rest of the world has still kept going despite the fact that you are broken. Sometimes you might think you will never recover and never get up. Still, you have dusted yourself off and carried on. If you have survived your world shattering over and over again and still you are here, you should be proud of yourself because it is no small thing.

There can't be one human in this world without a problem. It is all in the way you look at it and change your way of thinking.

<u>Let us understand the concepts in depth:</u>

What is a Problem?

A question that is raised for inquiry, consideration or solution. An intricate unsettled question. A source of perplexity, distress or vexation. Difficulty in understanding or accepting.

What is solving?

To find a solution, explanation or answer. To fix a problem we need to solve it by finding a solution.

What is a Solution?

An action or process of solving a problem. A bringing or coming to an end or into a state of discontinuity.

Note before Problem Solving:

* Be proactive and not reactive.

* Calm down and stop worrying

* The problem is already here and it has happened. So stop discussing the past.

* Allow your brain to think to find possible solutions.

Paradigm shift and thinking:

Think about the issue from so many different angles, from another person's point of view. Put yourself in other's shoes. While thinking… try to answer the questions related to Why? When? What? How?

- Why is the issue coming up again and again?

- When was the last time I felt this way?

- What can I do to stop this problem from recurring?

- How can I handle this situation in a positive way?

Once you start questioning, you would have already started thinking about the solutions and you can sense your mind getting calmer. You will gain the confidence to tackle the situation no matter how big or small it may be.

17. APPRECIATION

As a positive psychology practitioner, I would say appreciation and gratitude are interlinked. Appreciation is linked with greater happiness. It helps you feel more positive emotions, enjoy good experiences, improve your health and build strong relationships.

You need to appreciate life even when it is not perfect. Happiness is actually not only about getting what we wish, but also appreciating what we have. We people spend a lifetime looking for more when we could have spent a lifetime enjoying what life has offered. We pray when we actually want something in life that we forget to thank and appreciate all that we already have.

Appreciation is the highest form of prayer. If you have a roof over your head, clothes to wear and meals on your table, you are probably the richest in the whole world. The more you learn to appreciate what you have, it stays with you forever and no wonder it multiplies that you can also give and help those in need.

The happiness jar that I have placed on my workstation does work wonders! Every time something pleasant happens in my life like - when someone calls, visits me or buys something for me, I write an appreciation note with loads of gratitude on a small piece of paper and drop it into the jar. Whatever I appreciate, it draws similar blessings in the form of people, love, care, affection, happiness and even money. By the end of the year on new year's eve, I sit down to read all those papers in the happiness jar just to feel blissful and also to attract more similar happenings in the coming year as well.

Appreciation has tremendous power to awaken one's soul and to make one more productive. A person who can appreciate you would give the spirit to achieve and to get going higher in life. Appreciation is the key to other's happiness as well as yours.

Every single human being has the deepest craving to be appreciated.

Being generous doesn't always mean giving away food, money or clothing. Being generous with appreciation counts too. We need to be grateful to people who make us happy. They are the charming gardeners who make our souls blossom.

You can appreciate each day by telling "It's a beautiful new day." Take a moment to reflect on the awesomeness of it. By doing so you are creating many more new beautiful peaceful days than a stressful hurry burry one. You may live your life like nothing is a miracle or live like everything is a miracle. The choice is yours!

Most of us run behind materialistic stuff and relationships that are not destined for us! Take a graceful walk as you live life. Live, enjoy and appreciate every moment of life to treasure them. Appreciation can make a day. It can even change a life. Your willingness to put it into words is all that is needed. Who knows? Appreciating could even be your purpose in life!

Have you felt the black spirit of envy wrap around you when someone is doing better than you at work or in life?

Well, that is a sign of a lack of appreciation of your own uniqueness and self-worth.

When someone is doing better than you, remember it is their talent and that each of us has something to give that no one else has. Appreciation is a gift we give to others. Happiness is what happens now when you appreciate what you have.

Appreciate where you are in your journey, even if it is not where you want to be because every season serves a purpose.

18. BEGIN WITH THE END IN MIND

"The seven habits of highly effective people" by Dr. Stephen Covey was one wonderful book that I came across. Begin with the end in mind is one of the seven habits discussed by Covey in his book. It means to begin each day or task with a clear vision of direction and destination and then continue by flexing your proactive muscles to make things happen. Covey says all things are created twice:

- **First in the mind and then**

- **In the real world.**

Physical creations follow mental ones, just like how homes are built according to blueprints. It means to start with a clear understanding of your destination. You should know where you are going, so you would understand where you are now and that the steps you take are always in the right direction.

It is easy to get caught up in the activity trap or business of life to work harder and climb the ladder of success only to realize it is leading against the wrong wall. You would be very busy your lifetime without being effective. Each of us struggle to get higher income and recognition, only to find that our drive to achieve the goal, blinded us to the things that really mattered the most and now are gone.

How different our lives would be when we really know what is deeply important to us?

By keeping the picture in mind, we manage ourselves each day to be and to do what really matters most. You will be truly efficient only when we begin with the end in mind.

Ask yourself:

- What do you want to do to this world?

- To the people around you?

- Am I a short-tempered person?

- Am I hurting my close circle with my bad mood and temper?

- How am I going to work on it?

- What is the purpose of my life?

- Why have I been sent to this world?

- What should have I accomplished before it is time to leave this world?

Time is short. If you have neglected these thoughts or postponed your vital tasks or the need of the moment, remember… the second best time to begin with something is now!

To make your desires into reality, you need to see and understand what those desires are. It is to visualize your life or career the way you want it to end up being. While I started making this conscious effort, I was able to take much control over my life, circumstance, and happiness.

Powerful words of Joseph Addison:

"When I look upon the tombs of the great, every emotion of envy dies in me;

When I read the epitaphs of the beautiful, every inordinate desire goes out;

When I meet with the grief of parents upon a tombstone, my heart melts with compassion;

When I see the tomb of the parents themselves, I consider the vanity of grieving for those whom we must quickly follow;

When I see the kings lying by those who deposed them, when I consider rival wits planned side by side or the holy men that divided worlds with their contests and disputes, I reflect with sorrow and astonishment on the little competitions, factions, and debates of mankind. When I read the several dates of the tombs, of some that died yesterday, and some six hundred years ago, I consider that great day when we shall all of us be contemporaries and make our appearance together."

19. TRUST YOUR LIFE

You can't go back and change the beginning, but you can start where you are and change the ending. One day you will wake up and there won't be any more time to do the things you have always wanted to do. Do it now! Trust your life and yourself. When life tosses you down, remind yourself one more time that you are not a victim for sharing your story but you are a survivor setting the whole world on fire with your truth. You never know who needs your light, your warmth and raging courage.

Your true character is revealed not by how you are on your best days but by how you act on your worst days. Beauty isn't about having a pretty face. It is about having a pretty mind, a pretty heart and a pretty soul. The real beauty begins the day you discover that you are such a nice person with compassion and empathy for people and towards life.

All of us break to pieces sometime in our life, but what really matters is how we get up and put the pieces back together. If you believe you have a healthy mind, then never speak ill of others... even those who tested and tried you during challenging times in your life. Nothing can be a good teacher compared to life. Going through sad experiences actually makes us smarter and through that we become better thinkers.

Life's challenges are not supposed to paralyze you, they are supposed to discover who you are. Always go with the choice that scares you the most because that is the one which helps you grow. Without rain nothing grows... so, learn to embrace the storms of your life. It is not about how many times you fell but how quickly you got up every time you fell. Jump when it is so scary to jump because that is exactly when you should jump. Otherwise you end up staying in the same place your whole lifetime.

Anytime you have thought about quitting life, remember that dying is a very easy thing; it happens in a single moment.

Living is the best challenge! While you sail through life, it is your choice to be a passenger or the captain of the ship. Are you going to react to every rising tide (problem) in your adventure or are you going to lead things in the direction you choose to move? The choice is yours.

Trust your life because life has put you exactly where you are supposed to be now. Look harder to find the higher meaning of your day, work or profession. If you are a teacher or parent, focus on the blessing you have got to shape the life and mind of a child. You could be the one person in that child's life to show him the path to success. Not everyone has this gift of working with a fresh young mind. Fill it with positivity and motivation to face the challenges of life.

- When the student turns back to see the path he or she has traveled, may you be the mentor who always has a permanent place in the student's heart.

- If you are a psychotherapist, counselor or life coach, you have the privilege to guide someone into light during dark days of their life. Give your hand to pull them out of the never-ending dark spiral that sucks them down.

- If you are a parent, do not focus on the sleepless nights, body change, weight gain, terrible two's, temper tantrums, sibling rivalry, academic pressure, pre-teen and teenage attitude. Instead, focus on the privilege of being a parent. Your children have come through you and chosen you as their parent for some reason.

See how you can be your child's best friend, guide and mentor during every stage of their life. Show them this place is not a difficult place to live in by boosting their self-confidence and self-esteem level. Grow them as the kindest person ever in the whole world.

Trust your life because you are here for a purpose!

20. PEOPLE WALK IN AND OUT OF YOUR LIFE

When you observe your life very keenly, you would have noticed that so many people walk in and walk out during every phase of your life. When you were young, you would have made it a point to stay in touch with your teachers, friends, crush and schoolmates, in spite of anything that happens in your life. But eventually as years roll by they would have vanished from your life without a trace and you wouldn't have taken an effort to have them back in your life either.

Life is like a train journey. You keep traveling no matter what, until your station or destination arrives and you will have to step out of the train one day too. Until then so many people get on your train from different stations and a few who have traveled with you get down in their destination when it is time for them. Still, your journey has to continue even without your fellow passengers who were so close to you. Maybe your grandparents, parents, friends, relatives, life partner, children, boss or colleague. We can't hold anyone with us forever. Nothing is permanent in this world, even people and relationships. Change is the only permanent thing in this world ever. A person who can easily cope with change, with acceptance and realization is the survivor and the winner to be. Losing our dear one and still having to live life in this so seemed empty world is very difficult. Your grief, tear and sorrow are not going to change anything or bring back the passenger into your train. You can still hear the train whistle in a distance. The train is yours and it is waiting for you to continue the journey with the memories of your people whom you carry in your heart with a moment of pride and bliss. It is not that we forget the sorrow or stop missing them as days pass by but we learn to live with the pain and their memories in our hearts. Every end is a new beginning!

A few places that our best people occupied in our hearts can never be filled by anyone else. You met them for a reason or a purpose and they taught you a few lessons and have left you in the place you are meant to be. If you really miss them and can't bear their loss… start living your life with a few pieces of advises that they gave you, follow their footsteps and live the journey as their little daughter or son. Feel proud you were given the opportunity to be their son, daughter, dad or mom. You were gifted to be a part of their life no matter how short or long the journey was.

There can be a few people who join your journey just to shower unconditional love and also to get the same back for themselves. I started believing in this with a few moments that happened in my life. The school and teaching profession gave wonderful moments. Showering love to all the students did bring back tons of love. It was a blessing rather than a gift when a few students told "Wish you were my mother mam. Your daughters are so lucky to spend more time with you." Wish I had many more moments of the students addressing me as mom instead of mam.

The moments my bestie's mom embraced me as her own daughter, showered unconditional love and affection to boost every single day of mine were moments that made me realize the love from people can make me a better person and embrace happy vibes too. Caring moments of sending me food, making calls, showering her blessings and when she calls me her daughter are memories etched in my heart.

A few students even after completing their schooling, visited me when they wanted some motivation to face their life or just a casual visit on my birthdays just to wish me! Akash surprised me with my favorite book on my birthday during the pandemic times. Rishi Varman demanded a closed pastry shop to be opened and got a birthday cake by around 9:00 p.m. I did have a wonderful 40th birthday and a memorable one too. I didn't fail to fill myself with thoughts of gratitude for having been blessed with such students.

We shifted to a new neighborhood and the new environment was quite new and were not aware of any known people there. I was fortunate enough to have an old couple as my neighbors. Their only daughter is married and settled down abroad. They were living life all alone helping each other. It all began when they cooked some food on their own daughter's birthday and gave it to me with love telling... you are our daughter too! That is when I realized their pure unconditional and started calling them *amma* and *appa*. The hot delicious Brahmin food hand cooked by amma herself filled my heart with warmth. Love is contagious too and it started going back to them when I packed food when amma was sick. What you give comes back in many folds… love and affection aren't any exceptions.

One of the best gifts you can give someone is a genuine thank you for being there in your life. Always remember, someone's effort is a reflection of their interest in you. More moments and more people are yet to cross my life and I can't wait to learn the good and bad lessons from them. Sometimes you can't explain what you see in a person. It is just the way they take you to a place where no one else can. Do crave to meet more people like them and be one yourself. Different people bring out different sides of you and there is nothing better than a good person. They can change your whole day and can change your whole life. Your life is not judged by fluent English, branded clothes or a rich lifestyle. It is measured by the number of faces who smile when they hear your name.

Life is ironic sometimes because we are loved by the most unexpected and let down by the trusted ones. While few ignore our faults to just see us smile, some make us cry for things that we haven't done. A few people stay with us even when we ask them to leave and some leave us when we need them the most. So, you need to know which hand to shake and which hand to hold because life is all about learning to hold on and learning to let go.

Be the person to push someone to do and be better. Just higher goals and motivation. Good times and positive energy can bring out the absolute best in each other. Good people you meet are like street lights along the roads. They don't make the distance short but light up the path and make the walk easy and safe. People walk into your life for a short period or a whole lifetime. When you are smart enough to know which one it is, you will know what to do for each person!

21. MATURITY

Maturity is a word that clings on to people who have gone through hardship and early life lessons. Or even otherwise maturity can be well-read from simple things in life. Maturity can also be about taking a knife, cutting the cord and setting yourself free from the immature back biters and fools. Maturity is to know it takes a minute to make someone's day and one word to destroy someone's life. Maturity is to know that your words have the power to hurt, heal, open minds and hearts and change the world and not to forget the responsibility you have over the words you speak. Maturity is when someone treats you like crap, but you realize it is because something is wrong with them and not you. Normal people like you and me don't go around destroying other people's lives.

Whoever is trying to bring you down is already below you. When you can forgive a person who wasn't sorry, that is strength and maturity. Ruling your mind and not letting it rule you is also maturity. The moment that you realize your mind is a treasure box to keep love, happiness and sweet memories, and discard anger, hatred, and jealousy is also maturity. A person with a pretty mind, pretty heart and pretty soul is a mature person. Maturity is when you can be silent, never respond to rudeness and don't take it personally. When others are rude to you, they reveal who they are and not who you are. What others think about you is not important. What you think about yourself means everything.

A person who knows to manage his or her anger is already mature. There is a huge difference between explaining your anger and expressing your anger. By explaining your anger, you will be able to right away open the door to solutions instead of arguments. Never mix bad words with your bad mood. You will never get the opportunity to replace the words you have spoken and you might not have a chance to explain yourself as well.

Leave everyone you met better than you found them. They might have a chance to learn something from you. Be a living role model! Everyone breaks at some point or the other. Maturity is to cry silently, wipe your tear and smile back again.

A mature person always has inner peace in spite of the turbulence around them.

<u>Symptoms of inner peace:</u>

* Loss of ability to worry

* Frequent attacks of smiling

* Frequent overwhelming episodes of appreciation

* Loss of interest in judging other people

* Tendency to act based on hope rather than fear

* Ability to enjoy every moment

* Ability to give and receive love

* Sharing whatever little you have with people having less in life

<u>A matured person copes up with change easily:</u>

Not many like change since it is difficult in the beginning. Change makes people look the other way or run the other way. The problem is accepting change and not viewing change as a process but as a situation.

5 Stages of change:

1. Denial

2. Anger

3. Bargaining

4. Depression

5. Acceptance

The 5 stages of change can be explained with an example:

There is an alcoholic who is on the verge of losing his family and children because of his habit. His family starts to break down because of his abusive behaviour when drunk. The family members who are concerned about the well-being of him and his family, force him to go to a rehabilitation center for a short stay for everyone's betterment. He would refuse to go and co-operate. This is the first stage - DENIAL.

He would be mad at the people who forced him to go to the center. The second stage - ANGER.

The alcohol addiction would make him bargain with people. Third stage - BARGAINING.

When he is denied access to alcohol, he gets depressed. The fourth stage - DEPRESSION.

There would be no other go and so he accepts the situation and begins to change himself for everyone's good. The fifth stage - ACCEPTANCE.

In any given situation of change, you can track your progress as you advance through these 5 stages.

If you are able to handle your own emotions, well that has something to do with your maturity level.

22. EMOTIONS

Emotion has a major role to play when it comes to being happier in life. Our life is touched in some way or the other by feelings or emotions. It may be the slight awareness of happiness or unhappiness which often visit us, or it may be one of the stronger emotion which enters frequently into our relations with people. If we can understand our own emotions and come to realize when they are good for us and when they are not, then we can use them to good effect in our lives. Emotion has a strong grip on us, it may be difficult or impossible for us to control. The trick is knowing how to use your emotion to get things done :)

Emotion for extra power:

Emotion at times is very important to give us extra energy that we need for physical emergencies. A young nurse with a thin physique has night duty to take care of a patient at the hospital. When the patient falls from the bed, under ordinary circumstances she couldn't have lifted the patient but filled with emotions of horror at the sight of the sick patient on the floor, she found the energy.

More examples….

* Parents are able to sit day and night without sleep at the bedside of their sick child. (love)

* Rescue workers who work tirelessly at a scene of a disaster. (compassion)

* A girl drives home on a lonely night, she changes the punctured tyre quickly and continues to drive home. (fear)

* A woman dashes into the traffic to pull a child out of the way of an oncoming car. (loss, compassion)

* A boy who knocks down an older boy who has just said something insulting about his father who helped him succeed. (love)

It is at such critical times that emotion may be one of our best friends and we would be lost without it.

Emotion as a drive:

Emotion is a strong motivating force. When there is emotion, there will be action resulting from it.

* Girl who is damn tired after the days work says to her mom "I will cook dinner tonight." DRIVE (love for her mother)

* A boy stays away from every school event. DRIVE (fear)

* A man organizes a big campaign to get the starving children fed. DRIVE (compassion)

* A man who energetically stirs up a mob to race violence. DRIVE (hatred)

Emotions and attitude:

Success in living depends greatly on having a good attitude. It is possible to live through all of one's adult life with attitudes formed in childhood and youth. The formation of a good attitude is as important to us as is the formation of good habits. One should be critical of his attitude and try to change them if they are bad.

Example:

QUESTION: "What is your attitude towards reading others mail?"

ANSWER: "I wouldn't think of such a thing."

That idea plus the feeling is the attitude. It is the feeling that you have revealed your true attitude. In this way, what will you do if you get a chance to come across someone else's letter? You will not read it.

Emotions and good living:

Emotion is important to our lives. It is a rich source of quality and color in our lives. Precious moments are those with happy and glorious feelings and emotions. Life is unbelievably happy when living with the glow of some happy emotions like love, the thrill of some adventure, warmth of friendship and pride in success.

Life is unbearable when in the depths of unhappy emotions like sorrow, despair, regret, anxiety and suspicion.

BOTH CONTRIBUTE TO GIVING LIFE ITS QUALITY!

Even the emotions often considered undesirable can be of great good. Think of how valuable rage and fear are if directed against injustice, greed and violence!

ANY EMOTION WHEN NOT GUIDED BY INTELLIGENCE CAN DO HARM.

Strong emotion provides less mental control at a time when it also provides extra energy. Anger does harm to the spirit and body. Other emotions may do equal harm too. Unkindness may make a child's whole life miserable. Suspicion may destroy a friendship. Hate or envy may start false rumors and tear down reputations.

What is emotional maturity?

One should grow up emotionally as well as in other ways. Everyone gets more mature emotionally as they grow older.

1. Controlling our emotions:

It is being in control of our emotions, having our reasons to approve our action rather than having only an emotional backing for it. It is important to be in a state of Poise. Poise means to hold in a balanced and steady position. It is an accompaniment of emotional maturity usually and it helps one to be in a state of balance.

2. Making proper use of our emotions:

Our emotional energy should not be the kind that burns and turns to ashes, but it should rather be the kind that burns and flows into action. In an emotionally immature person, emotions too often give just heat and not energy. Such a person will be filled with sympathy for the slum dwellers, but he wouldn't use that energy for action.

3. Being aware of your emotions:

It means being conscious of whether or not you are acting on the basis of emotion or thought. You may be depressed and discouraged and life may look hopeless, yet if you can be aware that it is an emotion that is giving your whole situation its unpleasant tone, it counts in as maturity. Now if you can look at the facts realistically, you will feel the situation to be comforting and encouraging. We may respond "I can't do it" when it is something difficult. It is the fear of the unknown that makes you respond so. If you can realize the emotion, you can see the situation more clearly and may find that it is something you can do with no great trouble.

4. Proper balance and fullness:

Some people have excess emotion in one area like sympathy towards a dog, getting hurt by someone when somcone fails to speak to them, constantly filled with fear, being too quick to become angry and always reacting to everything with a feeling of risk. It is important to strike a balance with your emotions. In contrast, there are people who are afraid of emotions and use too little of them. They feel little warmth towards people and know little of the joy of giving and receiving emotion. Some are more emotional than others. They keep a calm and unruffled exterior no matter what is boiling inside and so we can't depend on appearances.

5. Is emotionality inherited?

It is a result of both inherited structure and environmental influence.

A] How are good emotions acquired?

Suppose your emotional life is limited and barren, try to:

a. Look for situations that might arouse desirable emotions:

Hunt around to look for people with whom you feel like making friends. Try listening to a different genre of music, try your hands on different art mediums, outdoor sports, activities, travel experiences and reading different book topics. Somewhere, something will give you an emotional lift for sure.

b. Get rid of emotions that prevent you from experiencing possibilities:

Get rid of your shyness that keeps you away from people or that prevents you from showing affection to others. Get rid of the fear that prevent you from trying many new experiences. Get rid of unreasoned prejudices that shut off many possibilities for enjoyment.

c. Act as if you have desirable emotions:

Act friendly whether you feel that way or not. Act generously even if it takes a great effort. Show sympathy towards those who deserve it. Be tender in your actions towards those who need it even if you do not have particularly tender feelings. When you pretend to have emotions you will be able to gain them sooner in the process.

B] How do we get rid of undesirable emotions?

1. Work it out:

To get rid of anger, hatred, depression, sadness or annoyance, you can go for a walk, play ball, or clean your drawers and shelves. Emotions give you extra energy. It is a good idea to use it up through physical activity. Physical action serves a double purpose, for it also takes your mind off the situation that upsets you and it gets you away from it. If you are a college goer and a hostelite who is feeling homesick, find the company of someone and take a walk. If you are feeling depressed, go out to play a vigorous game of tennis. When you are done, you will find yourself in better spirits for sure.

2. Sublimation:

The redirection of thought and energy or the use of them in good activities so that they will not be used badly. Learn to divert your emotion from its unacceptable form to one that is considered more acceptable at home or in society. A mother who is stressed with the day's chores can divert the unacceptable behavior that arises out of stress to do gardening, artwork, reading a book or any activity like decluttering the home.

3. Stare it down:

Stare it in the face of bad emotion, recognize it for what it is and learn to relax. When you hear a speaker who makes fun of something you have long believed in and if you pay attention to yourself, you may feel anger rising in you. If you make an effort to relax and dispel it, you may be able to get rid of this feeling. Muscle gets tensed usually accompanied by unpleasant emotions. If you can relax the muscle tension, the emotion can be relaxed too. Notice how your arms, legs, and forehead feel when you are in such an emotional state. If you feel tension, focus to relax.

4. Get away from the source of unwanted emotions:

If you can't control your emotion in any way, get away from whatever is stimulating you. It could be a sibling teasing you, or your work might not be going well. Take a 15 minutes break. If the thought of tomorrow's exam worries you in spite of your good preparation, try to get your mind on something else.

5. Find a new response:

If a situation habitually calls forth undesirable emotion, try to find a new response for it.

* If someone arouses jealousy in you, find qualities in him that you can like and enjoy. Try to appreciate more of yourself so that you won't feel the inferiority that brings on jealousy.

* Shyness to talk to a group. Make it a point to meet people often enough that you can be smooth and self-assured with others.

* A soft answer will put off the fire. It is a normal tendency of people to return anger for anger. Try making a tactful response that will ease the other person or say nothing at all.

* If something fills you with anger, try to get outside yourself and see something funny about the whole situation. Humour is not only a wonderful substitute response, but it is also a wonderful tonic. Laughter is certainly relaxing and does us good.

6. Act the part:

Try acting the part as if you didn't feel the emotion. Acting as if you didn't have the emotion may make it disappear.

* If you are angry, try to stay calm and pleasant in your outward appearance. It will help.

* Assume a virtue whether you have it or not. Try to look like what you want to be and you would have gone a long way towards being what you want to be.

23. EXPECTATIONS HURT

Expectation means "an awaiting"

Expectations are a product of our imaginations. It is believing that something is going to happen one way, only to find that it doesn't always turn out the way we wanted. That is when disappointment occurs and drives us to feel a certain way about the situation. Human beings naturally feel that their fulfilled expectations will bring them happiness.

Having great expectations means, you think something good will come your way but if you can keep your expectations low, you won't risk being disappointed. Sometimes we set our expectations high. You might have mapped out a perfect weekend with your partner, a leisurely Saturday morning breakfast, spending quality time with close friends, then visiting your favourite place with your kids and finishing off with a delightful Sunday lunch. But you wake up to find that one of the kid is unwell or the car suddenly breaks down. When things don't go your way, you are upset and mad. These are called unrealistic expectations.

Change those unrealistic ones into realistic ones by choosing to set yourself achievable goals. When it comes to work or chores, setting yourself impossible goals is a bad idea all around. You will be setting yourself up for failure and disappointment in equal measures.

So what should you do differently? Instead of focusing on a whole day of entertainment, make one at a time… maybe walk to the nearby park with your family and have dinner at your parent's place.

I write down a checklist of the things I know I CAN DO. Instead of believing you can clean the entire house today, aim to spend three hours cleaning. And when the timer is up - stop! I survive by having a plan B sometimes to cope with my expectations. I would say there could be nothing wrong with having a backup plan C as well!

How to let go of expectations?

1. Discover your motivation:

Figure out the reasons behind your action. If you are honest and true to yourself, you are already past the first hurdle.

2. Consider your ideal outcome:

Think about the polar opposite. What would be the absolute worst outcome? Does it really matter if this is the outcome?

3. Form a plan B:

Try to have an alternative or second choice option. This will help you to move on if you are not able to achieve the gold standard outcome.

4.Say what you mean:

Words can be powerful, so choose them carefully and ensure they come from the heart. A few years back when I use to plan any weekend family outings, it would always end up with nothing. Either one of my friend would have a different plan or my bestie would have emergency cases. I can still feel how miserable I felt not being able to plan for a meeting and I would say what I didn't mean at all like "I am a failure when it comes to planning and my plan always sucks when it is friends meet". Though I was perfect at planning things, that moment of irritation made me speak things that I didn't mean. Later I realized I was able to attract more plan failures just because of what I thought and said to myself. I attracted what I told I am.

5. Realise nobody is perfect:

Even with the very best intentions, sometimes you will find yourself feeling annoyed with somebody. That is ok, we are all humans, so don't give yourself too much of a hard time. Just take time to reflect and work out what you could do differently in the future. And if somebody else is annoyed with you, remember they are humans too.

How to let go of expectations in life?

1. Acknowledge your disappointment:

If you are disappointed, allow yourself to be disappointed without trying to blame anyone else for the way you are feeling. It won't make you feel any less disappointed. Hopefully it will allow you to see the bigger picture. Acknowledge the way you are feeling and move on. Besides, there will be another time to do all the things you were planning to do.

When my second daughter Ela was in her second grade, we had taken enough training for the oncoming clay modeling competition at school. On the day of the competition, I was packing lunch and getting breakfast for the girls. I asked Kandharaj to keep the clay boxes in her school bag. Once she left for school, I noticed that Kandharaj had left behind one clay box out of the three while packing. By the time I found it the competition was already over and when I picked Ela back from school, I called up Kandharaj to inform him about the forgotten clay box. After a while, he called me back to see if I was mad at him but instead we gave him a surprise by telling "We are at the ice cream parlor celebrating the failure and it is so much fun than celebrating any victory :))"

That day I learned to acknowledge my disappointment and didn't blame my husband. Also I was able to teach my little girl a big lesson that good and bad times happen but it is all in the way we look at things and handle them.

2. Think about things differently:

When your plans don't work, we often tend to think about what we are missing out on. But negative thoughts like this can be a fast track to make you feel disappointed or even irritated. This is where you need to take control and choose to think about things differently. Try to view setbacks with optimism rather than pessimism. Focus on the things you are doing and enjoying, rather than the things you feel like you are missing out on.

3. Work out what you want:

Our friends, family and partners are not minded readers. You have to communicate what you want with the people you love, rather than expecting them to know. So if you want a Friday night out with friends, make it happen. Keep your better half aware that they need to be around to watch the kids. Do whatever you need to make it happen - contact your friends and arrange for your partner or your in-laws to take care of the kids.

4. Remember, only you can choose how you react to situations:

While you can't take complete control of what happens in your life, you can choose and control the way you react. The next time when things don't go your way, consider making an active choice to let go and move on, instead of wasting time, energy and dwelling on your disappointment.

Sometimes you lead to your own heartbreaks through expectations. Expectations are painful when you expect from the wrong people. You often forget what you expect from a person who doesn't care about you. Not everything in life will go as you expect. This is why you need to drop expectations and go with the flow. Don't blame people for disappointing you, blame yourself for expecting too much from them.

When you remove expectations from people, you remove their power to hurt your feelings. To be clear, expectations are not what hurts, it is the unfulfilled expectations that hurt most of us. The biggest secret to happiness is to have low expectations. Expect more from yourself than from others because expectations from others hurt a lot, while expectations from yourself inspire a lot. That is life!

24. ACCEPTING GOOD AND BAD TIMES

If you notice sharply, you tend to pray more when you are in bad times, when you need something desperately in your life. When you are happy and contented with your life you forget the creator. How many of us have the habit of thanking God for what we already have? We are happy and praise God when we are contented. But when bad times toss us, grill us and throw us on the floor, we curse God telling he is merciless :) Have you done that?

Life, the river always rubs on both the banks... happiness and sadness. That is the way life goes always. Good and bad times are part of your life and a blend of both makes life interesting. The paradigm shift of looking at bad times as your lesson to learn will eventually make you accept good and bad times the same way.

You will appreciate life waiting for both with the same mindset. It has got to do with more positivity during bad times that you have to look a little harder for the lesson and that little good thing hidden during bad times. When you go through bad times, God has nothing to do with it and everything happens purely by our Karma. What we sow we reap. It takes both good and bad times for your life to grow.

To remember during bad times:

• Everything can and will change

• You have overcome challenges before

• It is a learning experience

• Not getting what you want can be a blessing

• Allow yourself to have some fun

- Being kind to yourself is the best medicine

- Other people's negativity is not worth worrying about

- You have a lot of strength as a person

- Anything is possible

- Great things take time

Every single person will have to face good and bad times. Pain always helps us to learn the essential lessons at that point in our path. Sad days help us to heal, deepen and grow. The road to perfection gives one innumerable lesson to learn. The most awakened person also faces pain and suffering, so they can learn the specific lessons to rise to the next level of their life.

I always believe that the bad times put us on a direct path to the best times in our life. It's just a bad day and not a bad life. Unless you go through bad times, you can't appreciate good times. You need to experience sadness to know happiness. Like how everything comes to an end, believe that the bad times have their end too. While good days give you happiness, bad days give you the needed experience. Both are essential in your life.

Bad times also remind you of the value of the good times. Have you noticed that your bad times can show the number of good people in your life? The depth and strength of any relationship are measured in bad times and not good times. Stay positive when life gives you every reason to be negative. Without the difficult times, you wouldn't be here today. You need to be grateful for the good and the bad.

Good or bad, they are seasons of life. It depends on how you take it and adjust to these seasons. And seasons do change. Bad times are the occasions a good learner like you would not miss.

25. POSITIVITY

Staying positive doesn't mean you can't be upset or sad, it just means you have to keep going anyway and stand back whenever you get kicked to the filth. A negative thinker sees difficulty in every opportunity. You have to be a positive thinker who sees an opportunity in every difficulty. The most attractive scent that you can wear is positivity. Being positive is asking for a time out to shed a tear, dust yourself and then get back on track to run the race as you have never run before.

A positive attitude can be reflected in so many situations like being happy through achievements, encouraging others, facing problems confidently, showing patience, aiming for success, not losing faith in oneself, not thinking about bad times, managing stress and not worrying constantly about problems.

Train your brain to stay positive:

1. Help others

The best way to help yourself stay positive is to help others stay positive. People need positivity the most when they feel low key. Never allow the fear of their negative energy to spread to you. Instead, approach them with your positive mindset to show the light during the darkest days. I have felt this so many times when I am myself in a low key but in spite of that, a counseling session for someone improves my mood as well.

2. Staying centered

Staying centered the whole day will help you stay on track in spite of the negative energy that eats your positive attitude. Nature walk, deep breaths, meditation or yoga keeps your mind balanced. I learnt yoga in the year 2009 and have been practicing the same for the past 13 years with self-discipline. A day when I miss yoga makes me feel guilty the whole day that I squeeze in the yoga routine anytime when my stomach is empty. Yoga, meditation and breathing exercises help me to stay positive the whole time making me happier and that reflects on my skin which stays 10 years younger than my actual age. As you can see, they are all interconnected and staying centered is a foundation for your health, happiness and positive attitude.

3. Stay Active

"An idle mind is the devil's workshop."

When your mind is focused on completing the task for the day, immediate goals or monthly target, negativity is powerless. Assign tasks and fix a deadline so you will work on it desperately to enjoy the feeling of accomplishment. My to-do list includes home cleaning, a new skill to learn, calling up or meeting a friend, visiting flower market, arranging the flowers, head massage, reading a few pages from a book, watching a movie, an artwork, decluttering my workspace or home, deep cleaning with the maids, gardening, getting my hand dirty with mud, miniature toy making and learning online courses. Sometimes, I do feel like this lifetime is not enough for all that I want to do!

3. Daily gratitude

Every positive thing in your life deserves a thank you note from your heart. Whatever we are grateful for will expand or multiply when your attention is focused on gratitude. Every time I see my pet dogs running, chasing and playing… I write down in my gratitude journal:

"With all my heart, gratitude for the perfect health of my pets. Thank you! Thank you! Thank you."

Make it your habit to maintain a gratitude journal and write down at least three things you are grateful for. It could be family, work, good night's sleep and rest, sunrise, good health, food, clothing, shelter, money flow, peace, prosperity, happiness, love, compassion, helpful maidens, or the time you get to sip a cup of coffee listening to music and read your favourite book.

5. Eat, drink well and sleep well

Your intake of food, water and sleep has a great effect on your mood and mental health. Vitamin deficiencies can cause declines in mental health that can lead to stress, anxiety, depression, addictions and other psychological disorders. People who are sleep-deprived will feel more irritable and angry. Avoid staying up all night and you will feel happier, friendlier and more refreshed each day.

6. Subconscious re-training and inner healing work

To have a positive experience on the outside, we have to uncover and release the past negative experience trapped on the inside. The journey of discovery from within has the ability to heal the original wound that could have been created from our childhood, a bad relationship or a traumatic experience.

7. Follow your passion

Make sure you are doing what you love. If your job or hobby involves something that makes you feel guilty or that which takes you further away from where you desire to be in life, it is time to switch it off. Being in alignment with what your soul calls for is one of the most important aspects of staying positive throughout life. Practice any art, music, acting, singing, dancing, painting, drawing, poetry, sculpting, essays, gardening or cooking. No matter how well or bad you are in it, it is not about gaining money and fame but to experience becoming, finding out what is inside you to make your soul grow.

Did you know that listening to 5-10 songs a day can improve memory, strengthen your immune system and reduce the risk of depression by 80%?

When you take up any passion of yours as your full-time job, you will never feel the work stress and you will never get tired of working on your passion by being more productive each passing day. When you write the story of your life…don't let anyone else hold the pen.

Positivity is the key to happiness. Train your mind to see the good in everything. Positivity is a choice. Your life's happiness depends on the quality of your thoughts. Your happiness can be boosted by focusing on positive things. You can check on your thoughts. More like replacing a negative thought with a positive one. This practice will help to rewire your thought pattern to bring more positive thoughts into your life.

The ratio of positive to negative thoughts is a major factor when it comes to overall happiness. Your brain is monitoring the emotional tone of your thoughts - too many negative thoughts will make your brain respond by creating stress and sadness in your body. When you add more positive thoughts, your brain will create relaxation and happiness.

My personality development workshop session would make the students list down their positives and negatives. The positive column should be heavier than the negative column. The next target of the student will be to work on the negatives. Becoming aware of your negative thoughts and feelings, and having worked on them for a few days will gradually reduce the negatives. You will be able to concentrate more on what you want to do without experiencing distractions of emotions and stress. This will make you more productive, energetic and happier.

To grab more positive sparks:

1. List happy thoughts

Take some time from your daily routine to list all the happy thoughts you can think of. List the people and places that make you happy like good friends, favourite vacation spots, childhood memories and more. List things that make you happy… puppies, babies, the smell of a new car, a sumptuous meal, a relaxed day by a pool, etc.

2. Beware of negative thoughts and feelings

For the entire week, pay attention to your thoughts. Whenever you find yourself thinking about or feeling anything negative or stressful, label that thought "unhappy". Don't worry if you have a lot of unhappy thoughts and feelings throughout the day. It is perfectly normal. Just pay attention and label them.

3. Follow with a happy item

After you label an unhappy thought or feeling, follow it immediately with a happy item from your happy list. You may pick one item to use all day long, or choose different ones each time you need them. Just bring that happy thing to mind for a moment.

Don't just wait for the negative thoughts to come along so you can think about something positive. Add to it by making a conscious effort to think positive thoughts for your entire lunch hour or during one of your breaks. Decide that you will only have positive thoughts while driving in your car. Force a smile on your face as you bring your happy thought to your mind. This will help erase the negative thoughts.

How to stop negative thoughts?

I practice a few ways to stop the negative thoughts and it has helped me out. When a negative thought comes up, tell yourself "It is not true" and visualize the image of the thought shrinking until it disappears. You can change your brain waves by spending 10 minutes a day practicing mindful breathing or visualizing positive situations instead. Your brain doesn't know what reality is and what is imaginary. Change your pattern of negative thinking overall by adding a new routine to your thought process through daily reflection, affirmation or meditation.

26. BE PROACTIVE

Being proactive refers to self-initiated behaviour to solve a problem before it has occurred. It involves acting in advance of a future situation, rather than reacting. It is all about controlling a situation by making things happen or by preparing for possible future problems.

If I were to attend a workshop in a different city, I would go beyond actually booking air travel, arranging transportation and booking a hotel room for my stay. I will mentally walk through the 2-day event, deciding in advance what I will wear at the function, which presentations I will attend and who will I seek out in order to maximize my opportunities. In the process, I might decide that I will need business cards, writing materials, and casual clothes for the Saturday night dinner and shopping.

It is no accident that a few people always have a spare pen to loan, a safety pin to offer, a band-aid, or a pain killer when someone is in distress. These are the people you turn to when you need a hairdryer or a list of meeting rooms or change for the hotel vending machine. They are also the people who are frequently selected as project managers, management trainees and group leaders. They are organized, punctual, productive and respected by their managers and peers.

Proactive people carry their own social weather with them. They work on the things they can do something about. A proactive person's energy is positive, magnifying and enlarging. Being a proactive person, you have lived by selected values. When a problem arises, smile peacefully, accept the problems and learn to live with them even though you don't like them. This way you do not empower these problems to control you. You will also know your responsibility and will not blame circumstances or conditions for your behaviour.

Tools and mindset used by a proactive person

1. Set goals

Sunday mornings are the best for me to plan sessions for myself. It is a must to set goals with deadline dates. It could be a daily target, a monthly target or a bigger goal to achieve in a few months. I not only put them in writing but I do schedule time in my planners to work on them. By doing this, I am helping to create my own future to face any unplanned events.

2. Block off time for important tasks and activities

I use my planning calendars to reserve time for priority tasks and activities. By being able to visualize the future, I am able to anticipate possible problems and act before they can occur. Just looking at a scheduled meeting in writing, I set my mind to thinking about things I will need for that meeting. I schedule my priority activities about a week ahead leaving unscheduled time each day for those important and urgent tasks and activities that pop up throughout the week. I may have to do some juggling in order to fit them all in, but I never allow a priority task to be replaced without first rescheduling it to another time slot. I never replace a scheduled activity with a less important one.

3. Use checklists

I make a checklist for all repetitive events or activities, such as workshops, travel, a menu for the whole week, tasks to do or reminders. These checklists will be updated if necessary after each event. If I miss something, it is added to the list so that it won't be forgotten the next time. Checklists save time, money and prevent errors.

4. Review results

I don't just follow through with planned tasks and events, but I follow up too and make sure the value received was worth the time and effort. This ensures that I am indeed completing 20% of the tasks that yield 80% of the results. I always question whether I am making the best possible use of my time.

4. Plan long range

It is okay to plan early because planning too late causes crises and time problems. Small adjustments made earlier will avoid large adjustments having to be made at the last minute.

6. Set deadlines

I do set deadlines for every planned activity. You must be aware of Parkinson's Law, which indicates activities will consume as much time as you have available for them. Setting deadlines increases efficiency and prevents procrastination. When you work with deadlines, you will realize that stress is avoided. Only unrealistic deadlines cause stress, allowing more time than you think the task will actually take. Also, this allows those unpredictable interruptions.

7. Maintain the right attitude

Though there are certain tools and techniques that proactive people use, a major part of it is their attitude or state of mind. It is a way of life! Proactive people plan out even a telephone call by jotting down the points for discussion. A homemaker can be proactive by making a list of items they need before going to the supermarket, or reading the instructions before assembling a swing set for their kids.

These practices can be developed and nurtured until they become habits. Practice with little things such as before going to bed, decide on what clothes you will be wearing for the next day's meeting. You may discover that some clothes need pressing. Every morning have the habit of mentally walking through the day. What time will you leave the house, where will you park, which job will you do first...? The more times you think ahead, the more comfortable you will become with planning. As you see your days running smoother with fewer crises and problems, the more you will be encouraged to be proactive in everything you do.

Proactive means acting beforehand. Taking action in the present will influence things, perhaps even the future itself. So practice those habits practiced by proactive people. Set goals and schedule time for priority tasks and activities. Use checklists. Review results. Plan long range. Set deadlines and continuously make adjustments to improve future outcomes.

You need to know about being a reactive person to understand being a more proactive person. Reactive people focus on the weakness of other people, problems in their environment and circumstances they have no control over. They focus on blaming, accusing attitudes, reactive language and increased feelings of victimization. If you are a reactive person, you will be affected by your physical environment. If the weather is good, they feel good. If it isn't it affects their attitude and their performance.

Listen to your language. Proactive language or reactive language:

Your language is often the best sign of the degree to which you see yourself as a proactive person.

When something doesn't go well and you are mad at the people and environment.

A **reactive person** would say:

"He makes me so mad"

A **proactive person** would say:

"I control my own feelings"

Your **reactive language** will be:

"There is nothing I can do" during the time of crisis,

But a **proactive language** will be:

"Let us look at other alternatives"

Monitor your language firsthand to know which side you are inclined to basically because most of you wouldn't realize that reactive language becomes a self-fulfilling prophecy. Though you don't mean what you say, u tend to make it happen by telling and believing something negative will happen. Reactive language makes you feel increasingly victimized, out of control, and not in charge of your life or your destiny. They blame outside forces, other people, circumstances and even the stars for their own situation.

Proactive thinking also helps one to save relationships:

Ella and Daisy were best friends. Daisy went to school and she saw Ella in the class. Daisy greeted Ella cheerfully and tried to sit next to her. Ella gave a rude stare and told her to go away. Daisy still believed it was a prank and gave a pat on Ella's back and told her 'Don't be funny". Ella was too annoyed by now and stood up and pushed Daisy's school bag to the floor. Daisy couldn't tolerate the sight of her bag on the floor. She scolded Ella back in anger and in no time the girls had an argument and the teacher had to walk in to calm down the girls.

Daisy felt Ella treated her badly for nothing that she had done. She decided to break their friendship and made a promise not to talk to her anymore. Two days passed and the girls didn't talk to each other. Ella didn't come to school for about a week. The teacher informed the class that Ella's mom who was terminally ill passed away. The way Daisy reacted to Ella for the past few days was reactive behaviour. After knowing the reason behind Ella's lost smile and irritability, Daisy started thinking proactively.

Daisy could have thought a bit when Ella didn't greet her and asked her to move away because Ella has always been happier and cheerful and that particular morning when the girls picked an argument and fought, Ella was informed about her mom's sickness and that she had only few days to live. Daisy began to regret and told herself I should have asked myself these questions earlier...

"She is a happy person but if she is not normal, well something is bothering her, she is my friend always, let she take some time and let me wait for her patiently. What could be bothering her which makes her behave so rude to her own best friend?"

If Daisy had been proactive and thought earlier she could have avoided the argument and caused less pain to Ella. Not only Daisy, but this whole world is too quick and reactive with people or situations.

There were a couple in my neighborhood who yelled at their worker who had gone to collect their kid's bicycle from the workshop and took a pretty long time to return. They suspected him to have purposely made the delay because the workshop guy had informed them that the bicycle was ready and the amount can be paid immediately. The couple didn't ask the reason for his delay but were just reactive.

And once they came to know that the cycle was not wiped clean, it took more time to clean up. The workshop person didn't have change with him and he was a physically challenged person too. So the worker took a bicycle from the workshop to get some change and make the payment. In this incident the reactive behaviour of the owner is clear, but if they had been proactive enough to think and ask patiently the reason for the delay, it would have been a win-win situation for both.

27. MUSIC, DANCE, YOGA, AND WORKOUT

MUSIC

You are driving down the road off to work, listening to the radio and a song flips your happy switch. Immediately you are in a better mood and ready to take on whatever the day throws at you. The magic of music strikes you and has a positive effect on you. When it comes to the human brain, there is more than one thing happening to the brain when we listen to music. When a subject listens to music that gives them chills, it triggers the release of dopamine. Dopamine is not only released during peak musical moments but also when we anticipate those moments.

GET A COLLECTION OF SONGS THAT WOULD MAKE YOU HAPPY INSTANTLY AND THOSE SONGS THAT ARE TAGGED TO YOUR MEMORIES.

Hearing a song from our adolescence brings back a flood of feelings and memories. Why do those songs have such a strong hold on our emotional core? Our brains develop rapidly between ages 12-22, so when we make a connection to a song during that time, it is a strong neurological connection. The massive rush of hormones associated with our puberty years tells our brain that everything is super important and that includes whatever music you were listening to at that time. That is why when we listen to a true throwback of our high school days, it is a powerful thing.

GET A COLLECTION OF ALL YOUR FAVOURITE HIGH SCHOOL SONGS.

We have always heard about positive thinking from psychologists and self-help gurus. But what about positive listening? Is there such a thing as intentionally listening to positive-sounding music to boost your mood? People listening to upbeat music can improve their mood and happiness in just two weeks. I have a playlist of random songs which will uplift my mood and spirit immediately. I play those tracks in my kitchen preparing breakfast for my family and have always felt it to be the best way to start my day.

GET A COLLECTION OF UPBEAT MUSIC TO IMPROVE YOUR MOOD.

Never hesitate to sing along while listening to your favourite songs. It doesn't matter if you have a good voice or sing well with the correct lyrics - all that matters is that how happy you can be listening to music. I also have this habit of penning down the lyrics of my favourite songs, memorizing the lyrics and singing along. The lyrics of a few songs do have an impact on the listener. It is all in the way each one of us enjoy the music in our own way and never fail to explore.

GET A COLLECTION OF SONGS WITH GOOD LYRICS.

When you lack motivation or energy to do your pending work, never hesitate to play music for a good company and you will notice that you will be able to complete the chores much quicker and with hell a lot of energy left to do much more work. Somedays post-dinner, I sulk looking at the kitchen and dining space which needs a big hand of mine to sort the vessels, wash them, toss food back in their respective place and clean up the station. My only best companion at that moment will be music which gives instant happiness and that happiness in turn gives the energy to work much quicker than the expected time.

DANCE

Dancing is fundamental to being human. Dance is an outlet for emotions and a form of escape. Dancers have higher energy, less tension and a better creative mood than before. A study conducted on women who had been diagnosed and treated for breast cancer experienced an increase in life satisfaction and a decrease in depressive symptoms when they participated in dance therapy. Dance has proven to aid those with Parkinson's disease as well. Sometimes health benefits were observed just ten minutes after the dancing began.

When we dance, our brain releases endorphins, hormones that can trigger neurotransmitters that create a feeling of comfort, relaxation, fun and power. Neuroscientists of Columbia University say that when we move in tune with the rhythm, the positive effects of music are amplified. A little secret to make the most of the music is to synchronize our movements with the beat, so we will be doubling the pleasure. Dancing has a positive effect on our mental health.

As we move our muscles relax to the music, it allows us to free ourselves of the tension built up during the day, especially the one accumulated in the deepest part of the muscle. And very well with your favourite song list, you can hit the dance floor anytime you want an extra dosage of happiness. Simply believing you are the best dancer with the most graceful moves ever will help you plunge into the sensation. This has a ripple effect and you can simply feel the after-effects of dancing even hours later to make your whole day. My daughters have always seen me dance like a lunatic, right from their childhood. I am satisfied enough to say I have created little memories in their hearts. When they grow up they will remember how we twirled and danced in our kitchen mostly after dinner time.

I have been practicing a 30-minute dance workout session twice a week. The dance workout has boosted my self-image, confidence level and radiant skin. Lethargy and irritable pain in my body has disappeared and I can feel myself happier and healthier with just a 30 minutes dance workout session.

YOGA, WORKOUT

I am a yoga practitioner for the past 13 years. 2009 introduced me to yoga after the birth of my third daughter. I was 29 years then and I never miss a day of yoga, the elixir of youth and have been blessed bigger by Yoga. I am 41 now and still have the look, appearance, and skin of a college goer. Thanks to yoga which has surely helped me with anti-aging or age reversal I should say. The younger look and appearance for your age are enough to keep you happier and radiant for the coming up years. Yoga has kept me flexible in spite of my age and I don't fall sick easily since my immunity is always high. A sick-free body, which is much healthier means a lot to everyone and also multiplies one's happiness many folds.

A complete yoga session with Sivananda Yoga center for a month has been a boon for my mind and body. I take this moment to share a few real incidents in my real life where people mistook me as Kandharaj's daughter and asked him if he has 4 daughters. Also when the doorbell rings, I drop all my chores and attend the door, and the stranger would ask me to call my mom. I would say he can tell me, but he would insist I call my mom. Sometimes it has been so annoying that I have to tell people 'I am the mom of this home and you got to tell me".

At times this was helpful in a way to avoid people at my doorsteps too. I would walk out and tell the person at the doorstep that my mom is not at home so please come later. No wonder they did believe me and left.

There was one unforgettable incident that happened at the voting booth. There were two policewomen who were talking among themselves looking at me from a distance and they approached me and asked how old I was. They didn't believe me when I told them I was 33yrs and still they asked me for my Aadhar card to confirm my age. I took a pride walk as the two ladies were talking among themselves in surprise.

My day begins at 4:45 am every day. I begin with 11 OM chanting's, mindful breathing, meditation, positive affirmations, 10 rounds of Surya Namaskar, all the asana, face yoga, neck and eye exercises. This whole lot would take a solid 2 hours. When I don't have enough time to complete everything, I make sure to keep my stomach empty before lunch or dinner to complete the left-out asana. If you can make a fitness goal with a variety of workouts, do pin it up on your workstation where you will see and get reminded until it becomes your everyday habit.

However old you might be, if you haven't got introduced to yoga in your life, never miss the opportunity to learn from any good yoga center and a yoga tutor.

Sometimes monotonous workouts could be boredom and so I have a variety of stuff to do for the week like, first two days of yoga, the third and fourth day will be dance workouts, Zumba and a bit of weight lifting, fifth and sixth day would be a 1-hour walk, staircase climbing and cardio exercises. Variety in a workout session will keep you excited and keep you away from boredom. Make it a point to have some form of exercise for your mind and body because once they are taken care of, your happiness is always with you.

28. ENVISIONING: MAKING YOUR WISHES COME TRUE

Any kind of printing will always have a blue-print first. In the same way before any good or bad happenings in your life, the blueprint is created in your mind first. When you complain that life sucks, I feel unlucky, my plans don't work, people misunderstand me, blue days are with me always… all this happens because you attracted them with your own mind and your thoughts. Negative thoughts do come up naturally but every time you monitor them, you can replace the negative thought with a positive one. You may envision whatever you want to happen in your mind as if it has already happened.

For example, you might want to complete your graduation at the best university of your choice. But it is a long way to reach, your parents might have to prepare extra funds to get you to your dream university. Never worry about how to get to your dream place or gather the amount. You have the magic of envisioning to make your dreams come true.

All that you have to do every single day until your dream comes true is find a calm place without external disturbance (it is best to do the envisioning in the same place) close your eyes and relax your mind by inhaling and exhaling at your own pace. Start visualizing the name of your dream university and you are standing on the campus, right there with your classmates chatting next to you, you can see your professors walking past smiling, greeting good morning in return. Feel the happiness spread through your whole body and nothing wrong with shedding a few happy tears in the process. The more you jump into the envisioning process, the closer is your dream. Continue envisioning the graduation day, feel the texture of the black robe covering you, the feel of the black hat on your head, listen to the crowd's noise in the auditorium and your name being called, the loud applause, and feel the pride and happiness in you. Right from the stage, you look down to see your parents seated in the front row with happy tears rolling down their cheeks, who have traveled all the way to see your graduation.

HEAR THE CLAPS, SEE YOUR PARENTS HAPPY FACES, FEEL HOW YOU FEEL AND ENJOY THE MOMENT.

All that you have envisioned now gets conveyed to the universe and it will start processing all that you have wished for by attracting the people, place and money. You should not have a second thought or doubt about whether it will happen. Just carry on with your routine chores and wait for the good day and news.

How many times should you do this envisioning? Make it a routine to envision until your dream comes true.

When is the right time to envision? The best time is immediately after waking up or before sleep because the subconscious mind is much more alert like a sponge that absorbs water. The envisioning is done before sleep, the time when your mind and environment are calm, will process the wish the whole night while you are deep asleep. The universe works and processes to attract what you want into your life. The thought which lingers in your mind before sleep is quite important because the moment you wake up the next day you will be reminded about the last thought that you had the previous night. The same way, you can envision the same the next morning before beginning your day.

I taught the first set of students at school to create a self-assessment journal, goal setting and envisioning. After the end of the class, a girl approached me and told me she wants to talk to me in person. She told me about how badly she wanted a new keyboard but her father wouldn't buy it for now. I asked her to have complete trust in her envisioning and wish for what she wanted. Ten days passed by and I had the girl's class that particular day. She walked into the classroom with so much happiness and her eyes were filled with magic.

She told me "Mam! My father got me the keyboard that I wanted and I am so happy. Thank you so much for teaching me the technique." I was so curious to hear more in detail from her. I addressed the class by telling one of your classmates had used the envisioning method and had got what she wanted in a short period. The girl was invited to address her classmates and I asked her to explain in detail how she set her thoughts and envision them.

She began so, "I imagined myself seated in my room and my father enters the room with a box. He tells me 'You asked for this for a very long time right? Here you go.' I opened the box and to my surprise, it was the keyboard I longed for and I felt the happiness wave spreading in and around me. I ran my fingers on the black and white keys and felt the keys under my fingers, later pressed the keys one by one and heard the sound emitted from each key."

The key points to be noted that were told by the girl are…opening the box, seeing and feeling the black and white keys, listening to the music and she actually lived and felt the moment of happiness. Having the same feeling of how you would feel when you get something or when something happens, draws the wish closer.

Using a vision board can be one more way of manifesting your wishes. The concept of using a vision board will be understood by reading this real story. This real story is one among the few which did surprise me! There was a man who always wanted to buy a house for himself. He collected a random picture of a villa from the internet. He pinned the picture to the vision board which was on his work table, so the vision board was in his eyesight most of the time. He believed it was his new home and started living in it, walking through the staircase feeling the texture of the wooden railing as he climbed the stairs, feeling the firmness of the floor under his feet, sunlight entering his room through the window and how he started his day in his own new home.

He practiced gratitude and thanked God for the new home that he had already got. After a few months, he was sent to another branch office in a nearby city. He was promoted and also got a handsome salary. With the ample amount he started looking for a new house and he did buy one. As he started arranging the new place, he unboxed the boxes one by one. When it was time to set up his home office, the big box which remained unopened was opened and he did pull out his vision board.

To his surprise, he realized that the picture of the house that he randomly picked from the internet was the very same house that he had bought. He didn't attract a similar house that he envisioned but to his biggest surprise, he had attracted exactly the same house that he had envisioned. That is the real power of a vision board. When you create a vision board, you may draw pictures of your need or collect pictures from the internet or old magazines too. Place the vision board where you would spend more time or in a place where you would notice often. The very important thing to note is that never fail to attach a deadline to it. Pin a date, time and year so the manifestation happens right within the time you mark.

<u>29. ME TIME</u>

Time is everyone's most valuable commodity but we don't realize it until one day your hair has turned grey, you have aches in your body, you are not active like before or you can't remember things better. You have 8 hours for sleep, 8 hours for earning, and the remaining 8 hours for relaxation, recreation or dedicated time for our big purpose. The three sets of 8 hours are the most vital ones since they have the ability to build or tear us down as we move towards our life's goals.

Each one of us should know what awakens our spirit and gives more strength or energy for the future. It may be a peaceful dinner, a walk, a sip of coffee reading a book, playtime with children and pets, or just watching a movie. Neglecting me-time or the quality time for ourselves can bring harmful results. We have to recharge our batteries before we burn out exhausted. During any working day of yours, your energy gets depleted doing more of the same monotonous work. A change with something new will attract your imagination and restore your needed balance. Me time can give you energy and happiness for even a month to keep you going!

Most of us are unaware that one can prevent the shutdown of our creativity, imagination and intuition. People think that time apart from productivity is a waste of time and that they could spend that time in a much more productive manner. Once you realize that me-time is the one that can boost your performance level and also your happiness, you will go for more of me time sessions. Never postpone when your body cries out for recreation or personal time. Like how food, water, and sleep are necessities, renewal or me time adds fuel to your journey to reach greater heights. Time spent on you is not wasted... instead, it is the best investment for your future.

New mothers with infants, who fight postpartum depression can use me-time as a remedy for their mental health and also rejuvenate themselves. I was a full-time mom at home with my three girls and once in a few days my mom would take them to her home and take care of my daughters one whole day. I use to crave a day like that just to deep clean my home, re-arrange stuff while listening to loud music, dance while cleaning, try a new artwork and of course I would munch some snacks curling up lazy on the couch watching a movie of my choice. That night when my girls come home by bedtime, I would completely feel charged and my energy exploding to take care of the girls and even to handle much bigger tasks. One day for myself would keep me effortlessly alive and energetic even for a month. It is not that you need one whole day to revive yourself but just an hour or two just for you will make you happier and stress-free.

Take care of yourself because nobody would. Respect your mind and body when it is seeking a break or craving some real rest. Learn to honor yourself when you need a moment for yourself. Psychology says every person needs one hour a day for self-maintenance. One hour out of the 24 hours is less than 5%, but it really does matter. The relationship with yourself sets the tone for every relationship you have. Enjoy some time just for yourself before you enter into this world that rushes. Mental health is just as important as physical health and me-time contributes a lot to your mental health and overall happiness.

30. CLEAN AND DECLUTTER

Studies have proved that women who keep their homes clean are much happier and relaxed. In addition, they feel lighter and brighter. I am able to keep the stress away on an overwhelming day just by getting the sight of my clean and organized home. Certainly cleaning is connected to the betterment of your mental health. Generally people try yoga, mindfulness or even a massage to destress themselves... yet only very few destress themselves by quick dusting, wiping the kitchen and organizing the table or closet.

Assuredly clutter and mess will have a direct impact on your mental health. Women with cluttered homes have higher levels of cortisol. Cortisol is the stress hormone that might induce rapid weight gain, high blood pressure, muscle weaknesses, and mood swings, anxiety, depression or irritability. A study by Princeton University researchers discovered that clutter can make it difficult to focus on a particular task. It was discovered more specifically that a person's visual cortex can be overwhelmed by objects not related to that particular task, making it harder to focus and complete tasks efficiently. Mess and clutter are linked to negative emotions like irritability and a confused state. An organized home brings more positive emotions like calmness. Above all your brain understands clutter as some unfinished business and this lack of completeness gives stress.

By cleaning and organizing your home, workplace, desk or even one drawer, you will be able to take control of your own environment and this helps you focus better on other issues in your life. Decluttering and cleaning gives a calming effect to your mind and body. A study by the University of Connecticut found that during highly stressful times, people commit to repetitive behaviors like cleaning because it gives them a sense of control during a chaotic time. When you feel an urge to clean while you are upset or stressed, it is a sign that your body and mind are looking for a way to bring some order inside and outside you. Did you even know that anxiety, mental health and clean house are interconnected? The clean house draws the best mental health and mental health in return can help you reduce your anxiety.

No doubt applying mindfulness while cleaning can have multiple positive ripple effects. I am mindful while washing the dishes. I take time to smell the soap and take in the experience of clean water running over the dishes and the sparkle of the dishes. It surely does reduce the stress on my nerves and I am inspired mentally for sure.

As an example, folding the sheets and keeping your bed has a big impact while beginning the day by making you happier and more productive. People who have clean sheets and keep their bed regularly can easily be morning people who can wake up without an alarm. Just by making your bed every morning you will get confident, adventurous and sleep well at night. You are accomplishing the first task of the day by making your bed. It does give me a sense of pride and encourages me to do one more task and another. That one task helps you finish so many tasks that particular day.

I have sensed my inability to focus on the to-do lists for the day especially when my home is messy, cluttered and dirty. Clutter can limit your brain's ability. You will feel less distracted, less annoyed, and more productive immediately after organizing your work area. Students or working people who have difficulty on study or working can try decluttering their study table or workspace. If you are a person who can't limit the number of possessions, well it is time you start to limit or encourage yourself to discard or give away things in your home that you really don't need or don't use. I make it a practice to schedule one day of the month for the clean-up and decluttering. Doing this helps me to declutter my mind in the process and it feels like I have more space in and around me. Clutter happens when you have an excess of anything like books, papers, toys, shoes, clothes, food or even antiques. Wherever the clutter may be, in your car, on your desk, in your closet, in the living room, just get rid of it. Things that occupy space in your home for no particular reason take up space in your mind too.

Cleaning is a big task but breaking it into smaller parts does motivate you. I have this habit of turning back before leaving any room, so I don't miss out on any used glasses, food plates, or items that don't belong to that particular room. This way I prevent things from crowding my home space and ending as a bigger task in just a few hours. Just imagine the plight of your mom or woman at home. If you are a family of four and each member contributes to pulling out 5 items and not putting them back in place, by the end of the day 20 items need to be picked by the lady at home and it sure does stress her. I can never tolerate the sight of a mess when I wake up every morning. I make it a point to organize my home before going to bed because the sight of a clean organized home the next morning is pure joy and just refreshes my mind and body to start another day.

As a family it is each one's responsibility to keep an organized home, hence make it a point to talk to your partner, kids and family members to help you organize the place where you live together. The place is your heaven while you live down here and home should be a place that makes you happy and calm.

31. DETOX

The best way to detox your mind and body is to take a technology break or it is also called digital detox. A short time away from your mobile or any digital device refreshes one instantly. You may begin by leaving behind your gadgets turned off for a whole day or leave your device at home while you go outside or take a walk. Sometimes you need to disconnect and reconnect for the best. Technology is toxic because we are over-dependent on it and we do prove it by driving while using a mobile phone and all of us pulling out an iPad or mobile phone at the dinner table. Technology has a negative impact on the connection with people. There is a slow drift in the families when parents bring their work home and students slip into the internet instead of opening their textbooks. Practice mindfulness when it comes to when and how you use the technology.

The next best and easy way to detox is by sweating. Sweating will detox your body through the skin, whatever exercise it may be. Sauna therapy helps to sweat out toxins. A relaxing massage enhances circulation and improves the body's natural detox system, the lymphatic system.

Other ways to detox your mind are yoga, meditation techniques, making a low-tech day, taking a relaxing bath, intake of enough water, sips of green tea or doing anything which makes you feel relaxed. Religious or spiritual needs shouldn't be ignored as well. You may meditate, chant shlokas, read scriptures, pray, go to church or temple, or just enjoy nature, but doing something to uplift your spirit is needed for balance. Take 10-15 minutes to meditate, read or enjoy some time alone before you hit the bed.

Detoxing your soul is as important as detoxing your body and mind. The first and foremost thing to do is to remove toxic people from your life. Who are toxic people? They are who prioritize their self-interest above everyone else's and they never consider another person's emotional state. Does this sound like anyone in your present or past life? If yes, do remember that these negative people never change and they will change only if they have a need. You cannot make them change and toxic people wouldn't admit their mistakes when they have wronged someone. If you still feel that someone in your life makes you depressed, anxious or you feel like you are not your true self when around them, well you should never go about doing things to keep them in your life. Toxic people will take away your self-worth, break your self-esteem, bring you down and can even make you sick mentally and physically.

Reduce the possessions, discard the unwanted then and there to keep only the things that you need. Maintaining a clean workspace and home space will clear away the clutter in your mind. Practice sitting in silence, away from this busy noisy world, detaching from life for a while for just 5- 10 minutes focusing on your breath. This simple practice will do wonders for your soul. Remember to treat yourself well. Once in a while take a break from all of your life's stresses, do things just to make you happier and that would recharge you. You do deserve it.

The real demon which slowly eats you is to be in a job that you don't enjoy or like. Most people don't like their job but continue to work anyways just to pay their bills and that is the push behind working at jobs they hate. Thinking out of the box with some research will fish the job that you will enjoy. You and I don't age to live forever, so make the most of your time and be courageous enough to do what you really love doing. Taking a job that you enjoy will give you less stress and you would never get tired of working on it for hours since you love what you do and are amazed by the result.

Furthermore we are living in an unnatural world, the creations of man will not give you the serenity that nature does. Take off from your normal routine to reset your mind and rejuvenate your soul by connecting to Mother Nature. Spend time in nature by taking a trek into the woods, mountains, bird watching, nature watch, a stay in a place surrounded by tall trees and birds chirping will always bring you back to form for sure.

A few people reserve a day just to cleanse their minds to keep away the past events that upset them by writing in a journal to push out the worries, emotions and regrets. You may even start a personal ritual of writing a letter like how I do. The letter doesn't need to be posted or sent. I begin the letter by writing "Dear dream journal" and spill out the emotions and thoughts that are piled up and those which occupy too much space in my beautiful mind. I never push these emotions away but instead, harness them and move on to becoming a better and smarter person than before.

32. FAMILY AND CHILDREN

Family comes first. A house becomes a home only with family, children, love and bond. People who have a family are much happier and more productive. Your family builds a worthwhile foundation for your emotional well-being. Family is the place where you actually get rejuvenated or charged up. Family is the first place where you develop self-respect because they encourage you to be kind to yourself, help you see the good qualities that you missed seeing and motivate you to take your talent to the next level.

People with family have a purpose to live and earn apart from earning for themselves. Returning from work, they have a warm place to get back to, his home, and his family, surrounded by warmth, love, affection and unconditional bond. The family will be the people who will never judge you and are those who would stand by your side even when the whole world is against you.

How many of us get back home from work with all the stress piled up inside the whole day and blow out the stress and anger on the poor innocent souls at home who have been eagerly waiting for your arrival? Maybe you didn't hear the sweet voices behind the door storming to open the door for you telling "Daddy is home". Whatever work you had the whole day or how much your boss grilled you, it doesn't matter. The moment you enter your home, you must keep all that aside and receive your kids and family with open arms telling "I am home". If you feel like you are not able to get the work stress out before reaching home, well don't reach your doorsteps before that. You may park your car in the parking lot, de-stress by listening to some music, or make a call to your bestie or anyone who would understand, just to vent out before going home. There are a few people whom I have seen who would drive some extra kilometers before reaching home to calm down their mood and go home as one perfect dad or mom. Figure out which way suits you.

People with family are better taken care of and looked after. Taking care of your body improves your mental health and that in turn makes you happier. The family insists on a few practices like having a healthy and nutritious diet, keeping away addictions like alcohol, smoking, and also insists one to exercise to get fit physically. Family is the one that cheers you all through your journey. Family is the first to point out when you gain weight. Never bounce back on them with a temper because your family cares for you, they need you, they need you healthy enough to live a long life and they don't want to miss your presence.

THEY REALLY LOVE AND CARE FOR YOU!

Spend more time with your family in spite of your busy schedule by going out on picnics, a meal together, or plan some family activity like board games or movie time. Laughter is the best medicine ever and you can count on your family to give you many reasons for laughing, having fun and happiness. Research on a group of retired people who had earned abundant income conveyed that by the time they turned back to live a life with their family, their children had grown up and left their home to live their own life, their life partner was old, feeble and realized old age had crept in, in the form of grey hair and wrinkles, had missed all the fun time of playing and reading with their kids and missed romantic dates and dinners with their life partner. The time not spent with a husband, wife, child or parent can't be bought with the money you have earned. Most of them regretted having not taken care of their fitness and health and all that they had earned goes for their medical bills. We tend to postpone things thinking we still have time to care for the family and children but one day you will wake up to realize that you have lost all the time to do the things you have always wanted to do. Do it NOW!

People on their deathbed never miss a job promotion, title or award from work. They don't even talk about the business deals they missed or the partnership. They just feel bad for working so hard in jobs that replaced them in no time once they retired or were dead. Regret is very painful and make sure you don't have one in the future when the days and years have slipped through your hands when you were not aware. Be there for your family like how they have been there for you, live every moment mindfully, talk to your teenager who is having difficulty coping and pull your wife out who might be in a depression she is unaware of. Take your kid on a private date. It's only you and your kid for a whole day with lunch, a movie, a long ride and peace talks. These would be the precious moments your child would remember and also etch in their little heart when you are not around. They will never know how hard you worked or how much money you paid for their education. They would only count on the time you spent with them, just for them and adore you as the ultimate hero!

If you are a homemaker staying at home taking care of the home, family and children, have you realized that in spite of your family keeping you on your toes to do errands for them, they are keeping your mind busy and healthy too? An idle mind is a devil's workshop. You are able to keep away yourself from negative thoughts and ideas by planning for the day, meal schedule for the week, keeping a clean home and getting presentable clothes for your children and life partner. This is not one easy job and it does require skill and you are getting better at it every passing year. Women are the pillar of any family and when she is shaken, the whole family is disturbed. You are the CEO of your family and take pride in it. If you observe keenly, your family members are your reflection. When you are happy they are happy too and when you are upset they get cranky too. It is very important to keep yourself grounded, calm, and balanced since you are the foundation of your family and do your work with love, care, affection and loving-kindness. Never forget to have your ME TIME, since you need your own time to keep yourself happy and recharged to take care of everyone's needs. Don't you think it is the world's amazing huge task which people like you and me do effortlessly? Of course, we need appreciation every single day but it is also okay to know our worth, raise and support our family with pride and smile.

Never look at your children as stress givers. They have chosen you as their parents and trust in you to appreciate and motivate them. Each child has come to this world for a purpose, a reason... help them discover their talent, potential and sharpen their skill. Never force your wishes and goals on your child ever. You could have not had an opportunity to get into the professional line, don't try to pressure your child to become a doctor or an engineer. Allow them to become what they want to be... a dancer, musician, athlete, gymnast, archeologist, astronomer, sea diver, artist or whatever they want to be. We often forget that our children came through us and not from us. They are a different unique soul who is here to serve this world in their own way. We can't force them to become what we like. Respect your children and appreciate them seeking their purpose. That is our responsibility as their parents. We need to protect, nurture and love them without any condition until they grow their own wings to fly and survive on their own. Your children will leave the home, their nest when they can fly... so until then cherish and live every moment. Be the best dad and mom you could ever be. Your children grow up in the blink of your eye.

I remember my mom's words "Suma your children will grow up and leave you in no time. So enjoy raising them and admire every stage of their life being mindful of every single smile and gesture of the little ones..."

The moment your child is comfortable enough to leave you, it means you have done your job as a good parent. They are not ours to keep and our job is to teach them to soar on their own. Being blessed with children and family is a gift that many don't get. If you have one to call your own... you are bestowed with one of the best gifts. Never fail to cherish them.

33. LIFE PARTNER

We need to talk about choosing and having a good life partner because 99% of one's happiness depends on the person you choose to live your whole life with. Your marriage should be the kind of marriage that makes your kids want to get married and live a life like you.

Choose a partner who is good for you and not good for your parents or your image. Your partner should make your life emotionally fulfilling. Do not be in a hurry to start a family or plan for children until u take enough time to understand each other and you get to know the other unexposed face of the life partner. So many people are stuck in marriages just for the sake of the children or for financial security. People pacify themselves by telling them things will get better sooner or later. You cannot heal in the same environment that made you sick!

When you can confirm that the marriage doesn't work and don't have kids yet, it is easier to take a decision and walk out of the marriage. Walk away from people who put you down or make you feel lesser. Move away from fights and arguments that will never be resolved. You can't please someone who never tries to see your worth. The more you distance yourself from things that poison your soul, the healthier you will be. A person who is stuck in an abusive marriage or domestic violence suffers from untold depression and finally becomes like a piece of log drilled by termites. A true caring loving partner takes care of all your needs be it small or big and gives respect. Your happiness should matter a lot to them.

Personal space is a must between the two in spite of being life partners. Independence and freedom are quite needed and one shouldn't control the other. You can't keep your life partner within your palm and interrupt each activity that they do, they are not your possession or object. He/She is one individual person who came alone and has all the rights to live their lives and have their own passions, likes and individuality. Love blooms only when there is freedom between two people.

Fights and arguments are common in any relationship but the time and way one resolves are vital. Anything should be a conversation and not an argument. Never go to bed without solving an issue and don't stay away and never stop talking to your life partner because we never know how long we have each other in one's life. Psychotherapists suggest couples plan for kids only when they can confirm they wouldn't fight anymore. Research says couples fighting and arguing during pregnancy days do affect the unborn child. It is a complete NO to fight, scream, yell or argue in the presence of your children.

A few are unaware of being in domestic violence though they have lived years of married life. The partner doesn't have to hit you or slam your head into a wall to label it domestic violence. They can degrade you, humiliate you, scream at you, blame you or hold finances or even just try to control you. It is still domestic violence. A few are ready to take anything and sacrifice their self-respect just because they love their partner. Yeah! Love is blind. When you see someone who reveals who they really are with their fit, rage, temper or harshness, believe them. It doesn't matter how much you love them, there is always a difference between being compassionate and being abused or taken for granted. Reach out with an open heart, be kind, loving and compassionate but never let anyone treat you less than you deserve. A true life partner will make you feel happier, valued, and worthy. If they fail to realize that, it is okay to close the window that hurts, no matter how beautiful the view is. It is okay to say goodbye to some people to say hello to your birthright, YOUR HAPPINESS.

It is never late to question yourself "Am I ready for a change in my life, Am I ready to change myself?" It doesn't matter if you are old, young or what you went through…you can always be born once more time. Repetition of days and happenings is an intimation that if change doesn't happen, make the change and be the change. Every breath of yours is a chance to be reborn and fix your life and happiness.

Convey what hurts you and when you feel you deserve to be treated better, demand it! Just in case a spouse is into addiction, and behaves violent and harsh, conveying to them is the first step. The way they respond to it is important. Either they would frown at you or make you believe it's not their fault and yours that, you misunderstood them. If at all they consider, rethink and observe themselves and realize a few of their emotions need control and balance, well then it is a positive sign. If they are unable to handle it themselves, figure out they need some professional help with counseling and therapy. That is how things work and happiness flows back into your life. Be that kind of partner who would push your better half to do better with no drama and negativity. Motivate them to achieve their higher goal and aim. Be the proud man or woman behind them. Share good times and positive vibes by bringing out the best in each other.

Do not accept sorry, commitment or trustworthy words without a behaviour change. Sorry without a change in behaviour doesn't have to be accepted. You have this one lifetime. How do you want to spend it? Regretting? Apologizing? Doing errands and running behind people who don't see you? Be brave and believe in yourself. Do what feels good and makes you much happier. Take steps for betterment, take risks and make yourself proud. It is okay to knock on the closed door a few times. If it doesn't open in spite of all your efforts, let it stay closed. Sometimes it is better not to change a full stop into a comma. Know it when something is over, really over and set your mind to move on.

34. CHANNELISING ANGER

Anger is one of the emotions which is an intense emotional state. Modern psychologists view anger as a normal and natural emotion experienced by humans. Uncontrolled anger can be compared to a wild animal which when let out will hurt the people around, ruin relationships and health too. Channelizing anger is the key. It is important to deal with anger in a positive way.

One should know ways to manage anger than regret it later. Make it a point not to talk about anything in the heat of the moment and think before you speak than regret it later. It is alright to take some time to collect your thoughts before saying something. This time will allow you to think clearer than before and once you are calm, express your anger and your frustration in a nicer way. Express your needs clearly without hurting others in the process and don't try to control them. When you feel like your anger is beyond control, get some exercise. Physical activity has the ability to reduce stress immediately. Spend some time doing any physical activity that you would enjoy like going for a brisk walk or running.

It is okay to take small breaks during a stressful day. Just a few minutes of quiet time will give a moment to prepare and handle the day or people without getting angry. Always remember that anger can't fix anything and might make things worse. You have to shift the focus to solving the issue that has been raised instead of focusing on what made you mad.

Using 'I' statements has always worked in my life. Instead of criticizing or placing blame, be respectful and specific using 'I' statements. Maybe your partner promised to help you with keeping and arranging the grocery but he didn't. You will have to frame the sentence this way,

"I am upset that you left the groceries on the table without offering to help with arranging."

Instead of

"You never do any housework."

Holding on to anger is like carrying hot coal in your hands. It would hurt you first rather than hurting the others. Practicing forgiveness helps one to learn from the situation. Without forgiving you will be swallowed up by your own bitterness. Forgiveness helps you feel better, lighter and healthier in a way giving way to positivity and happiness. Forgive for your sake and do not hold any grudge.

A few find humor helpful to diffuse their tension. Humour helps to make you face what makes you angry in a way. But avoid sarcasm, it can hurt feelings. Practicing any relaxation technique when your temper flares up is handy to cool oneself. It can be anything you are comfortable with like listening to music, taking a few deep breaths, imagining a relaxing scene, repeating a phrase to calm you down like

"I am cool, take it easy", or writing down in the journal or even striking a few yoga poses.

In spite of trying ways to channel or vent out your anger, controlling anger is a big-time challenge for everyone. Never hesitate to get help for anger issues if you feel like your anger seems to be out of control or makes you do things that you regret later. If your anger hurts those around you, you should get help. Unmanaged anger can cause harm to your body and raise health problems like headache, insomnia, high blood pressure, depression, digestion problems, abdominal pain, anxiety, skin problems, heart attack or even stroke.

People tend to express their anger in inappropriate harmful ways like anger explosions or anger repression. Those who find it difficult to control their anger explode in rages. Raging anger often leads to physical abuse. A person who finds it difficult to control their temper should isolate themselves from family and friends. Those with low self-esteem use their anger as a way to manipulate others and feel powerful. Anger repression happens when people think anger is a bad emotion and choose to suppress it. Bottled-up anger becomes depression and anxiety.

Learning to express anger is a must for everyone including children. If your children get angry easily, are harsh with words or action or tend to throw things in their temper, well one of the parent would have been so. Children learn from their parents or from the people with whom they spend most of their time. Children learn from you by observing the way you handle a situation and channel your anger. Practical problem-solving skills can be taught right from childhood days. Children should know the difference between aggression and anger. Teach those different ways to calm and soothe themselves.

35. LOVING KINDNESS

METTA MEDITATION

I must discuss about that one book from my collection on anger management. The book's name was **CURBING ANGER, SPREADING LOVE**, written by Bhikkhu Visuddhacara.

I would love to share a few important topics from the book which have helped me enough to manage my temper and become one loving person to all beings. Metta meditation is the key to handling anger. The whole book speaks about four simple lines that have enormous power beyond imagination. The lines have the magical power of tuning a person's subconscious mind. Just in a few days you can sense that you don't get angry in circumstances where you would flare up.

What is Metta? Metta means loving-kindness. Just a few days of radiating loving-kindness using metta meditation brought about a big change and in one circumstance where one of my maid was so rude with her words and actions, I was so calm and serene that I didn't feel the anger or rage in me though. I would have reacted to the situation in a different way before the metta meditation practice. The maiden lost her temper and walked away leaving behind me in an undisturbed state of loving kindness to forgive her and allow her to peacefully leave my life. I have the habit of feeding the stray dogs in my neighborhood and after the metta practice, I got to see so many new dogs in our area who approached me like they were dragged towards me. They didn't ask me for food, they would just come close to me wag their tail like it would fly away, look deep into my eyes and converse something in their doggy language and just walk away, leaving me filled with loving kindness radiating and flowing.

On one more occasion, my pet dog Cinder went for a walk while it was raining. It is a usual habit to wipe his tiny paws before entering the home. Not sure if one of his paws was sore and when I tried to wipe it clean he did bite me, his teeth sank into my palm but still I suffered no pain. Incidents like these made me realize the mighty power of metta meditation. Recently we had the first water apple fruit yield from our home garden, the fruit was on the dining table and was just eager to taste it. So, I took a bite without noticing the red ants in it. Nearly after a minute had gone by, I felt a stringy texture in my mouth and couldn't remove it in spite of trying. I had to use my fingers to figure out what it was and pulled out so many ants still biting on me. I felt no pain or sense the ant bite even once. I didn't suffer any pain or swelling even after removing the ants!

Before learning the 4 magical lines it is vital to know what the effects of metta meditation are:

1. **You will sleep easily:** It's a cure for insomnia and you will be able to stop taking sleeping pills. You can radiate the metta practice until you sleep. You are promised to get a comfortable sleep without tossing, turning and also snoring.

2. **You wake up fresh like a flower:** You wake up ready to face a new day bubbling with optimism and cheerfulness.

3. **You would not have bad dreams:** Bad dreams like being chased by creatures or falling off a cliff or into a hole, or being haunted by ghosts are out of your way. Instead you will have pleasant dreams like flying through the air and auspicious dreams like making offerings and seeing beautiful sights. You might even have a sound sleep without any dreams.

4. **You will be dear to human beings:** People will like you because of your habit of radiating love and you will not have enemies. You will be able to make friends easily and also get along well with others. People around you will feel the positive mental energy or vibrations of loving kindness which is always radiating.

5. **You would be dear to every being:** Bhikkhu Visuddhacara says even spirits and animals will relate well to you. He

narrates an incident that occurred during Buddha's time. A group of monks meditating in the forest were disturbed by some spirits. The monks fled to Buddha and he advised them to go back to the forest and radiate loving-kindness. The monks did so and the spirits not only stopped their haunting but also protected them. The spirits even swept the monk's resting places and prepared warm water for them. The monks attained Arahatship at the end of their three months stay in the forest.

An old monk in Burma who is well known for his metta practice recollected how a swarm of angry bees were attacking people all around but not him. Bikkhu Visuddhacara recollects one   more incident of a sparrow flying towards a monk and landing on his shoulder. The bird rested a while before flying away while the monk was doing intensive metta meditation.

6. Devas will guard you: When you are dear to the devas, they will protect you. When devas protect us, we may escape from dangers. So a metta practicer is well protected. This is the true protection one should go for instead of seeking charms and talismans. Goodwill inevitably begets good.

7. Fire, poison, and weapons do not harm you: The Visuddhi Magga has mentioned two incidents that occurred during Buddha's time. One was the case of a woman devotee Uttara, who had hot oil poured over her by another woman who was jealous of her. But she was not scalded. The hot oil felt like cold water to her. The other incident was about a seven-year-old monk, Sankicca. Some robbers waited to kill him to offer him as a sacrifice to their Gods. But when they struck him with their swords, the weapons just bounced off the monk. The blades could not cut the monk. Amazed and awed, the robbers fell at the feet of Sankicca for forgiveness and were converted to the dhamma. There was also the story of a cow that was giving milk to her calf when a hunter threw a spear at her. The spear bounced off the cow because of the consciousness of love for her calf. The power of loving-kindness is beyond limits.

8. You can concentrate easily: The mind which is sunken in loving kindness can quickly concentrate. You wouldn't feel sluggish. This is because meditation helps to collect the mind and purify it, making it one-pointed and wholesome. In the long run, aimless wandering of the mind and distraction are controlled. You will be able to do your work with much concentration and focus.

9. Your facial expression becomes serene: Loving-kindness practitioners have that kind of beauty on their face that comes from their heart. Even if one may not possess fine physical features, you will have a kind of radiance and serenity that will be attractive and cherished by people.

10. Peaceful death is assured: Just as we live well, we must die well too. To die well means to die calmly, mindfully, peacefully, without fear of attachment, tears and sorrow. A practicer of metta who lives with a full heart of love for living beings would be living well, a moral life filled with love and expresses the same in his words and deeds. Consequently when the time for death comes, he is ready. He is calm and peaceful. When he reflects on his life, he would have no regrets about having lived a life of love and morality. Visuddhi Magga states that he passes away peacefully as if falling into a sleep.

The practice of loving-kindness and mindfulness can be a powerful combination. We will gain better concentration in our daily tasks and would worry less and live more lightly and cheerfully.

May all the beings remain free from harm and danger

May they be free from mental suffering

May they be free from physical suffering

May they take care of themselves happily.

PRACTICING METTA

Sit in your usual meditation posture, cross-legged on the floor with your back straight or on a chair, if you find it difficult to sit on the floor. Close the eyes and keep the body relaxed and recite the four lines mentally. You need not recite aloud or verbally. Keep reciting any number of times... it sort of programs the mind with thoughts of loving kindness and goodwill for all beings. One will be filled with the feeling of harmlessness, you will have no anger or ill will against anyone. It is a beautiful feeling.

You may radiate loving kindness as long as possible, for days and nights while sitting, walking and even during daily activities such as eating, bathing, washing, etc. You can radiate from 10 minutes to an hour after waking up in the morning. Even five-minute radiation of metta is better than no radiation at all. In the course of the day, as you do your daily chores, you can radiate anytime and anywhere. You can radiate metta until you fall asleep.

I am ever grateful to Bhikkhu Visuddhacara for the gift of Metta meditation. After all we have to prove to God that we are loving people with unconditional love for all beings and this is the purpose of everyone's life. Metta meditation is one simple and effective way to conquer loving kindness in this birth of ours. I have been given space on this planet and it is a magnificent gift to be born as a human. How can I pay back to mother earth?

Selfless love is the rent I pay for living on this wonderful planet and I feel contented and don't have any hatred once I started practicing loving kindness with everyone I meet. You don't need tremendous power to do things, just a dosage of love is enough to get everything done. You rise by lifting others with loving kindness and be a person who cares for everyone. Love people without hesitation and make someone feel seen. Make a difference in their life after they met you. Even when this world hasn't been kind to you, continue to stay soft and spread loving kindness. Be a light in this too often dark world.

I want to live a life spreading love and kindness that when my children think of love and kindness, they think of me. My success and yours are measured by how we treat people, our family, friends, colleagues and even strangers we meet. Spread the language of love and serve the purpose of your birth.

36. SMALL TARGETS

Achieving goals gives one happiness and a sense of accomplishment. Targets are of two types – short-term and long-term targets. Long-term targets fairly take their own time. Depression may set in when the progress is too slow or the task is too difficult. Setting small achievable targets and reaching them will give you a sense of well-being. It does increase your pride, happiness and contentment.

It is important to have small targets along with big ones to keep your emotions positive. Dopamine levels tend to increase every time you set goals and achieve them. It encourages you to keep going in life with a sense of pride and achievement. It makes you feel good and that is more vital. The way your achievement makes you feel is the need of the hour. Small targets and achievements improve your mood and self-esteem level. Keeping your self-esteem level high and checking on it goes hand in hand with your happiness and how you feel. Take time to celebrate every time you accomplish a goal.

Set small targets like working on a portion of your garden, cleaning you work station, rearranging a book-shelf or snacks corner, having coffee with a friend, improving self, getting fit, enjoying life more, losing weight, helping others, saving money, more family time, being a loving person every day, caring for everyone, morning wishes to everyone you come across, goodbye hug to your children every day, waking up a little earlier every day, to stay happy and positive the whole day, watching one emotionally fulfilling movie per week. It may be anything that you can easily achieve and so you can check your happiness scale and maintain it.

37. FACING FEAR

It is very common for people to avoid activities that trigger fear and only very few know about the intensity of joy and happiness behind facing their own fears. I would encourage you to talk about your fear. The more you feel free to handle your fear, the more hidden shadows are brought into the light and it is quite easier to be examined and released, leaving behind a happier you!

Of course, it is a daring move to talk about your fear. It is more like inviting the monster who lives in the basement to your zone for a coffee and chat. Once the fear is brought into the light of your awareness, it begins to dissolve and vanish at one point in time. Fear is not actually there, it is created by you and in the long run they start ruling your life. Your fear makes you feel small, not capable, chains you in darkness and makes you believe you are not worthy.

You must be ready to jump when you fear the most in life, take chances and draw courage to take the big step which is a stepping stone for a big future and dawn. Fear not because trust me...only fear will lead you to a new world, new people and new choices. It is a new world of freedom and happiness.

The other side of fear will always have success and pure happiness and you will find the person who you truly are. Discard fear of success, fear of being unique, fear of failure, fear of being rejected and fear of meeting expectations. You are born with abundant talents that you never know just because you didn't meet your fears. All those successful people are the ones who have faced their fears and passed through them to discover their true selves. You are just one step away from your successful days. Walk to the zones that frighten you, do not run away from your fears and instead learn to embrace them, travel with them, and dare to face them because the other side of your greatest fear lives your greatest life.

If you say I don't feel any fear on a daily basis, well I feel sad to say that you are living in your comfort zone clinging to the shoreline instead of wading through the fearsome waves to reach the biggest life waiting for you. Walk to the places that scare you the most and take some risks in your life to make some progress in your life. Fear makes you feel alive and it is proof that you are alive. When you gather the courage to travel alone and that very thought of it makes your heart beat rapidly, it means you are truly alive. Moments before addressing a large crowd, the feeling of butterflies in your stomach is proof that you are most alive!

Never allow fear to have arguments with your mind. Fear means you are alive, you have to accept it and walk through it. Fear is a beautiful indicator of your weakness and the area of your life where you need to get stronger. It is a great opportunity to know your fear just to face it, fight it and win over it. We have taken this life to face a few fears to instantly step into the next phase of our life, a wonderful life hiding behind each fear of yours that you are yet to face.

I have to talk about the fear I faced and how I became a speaker to motivate people in different gatherings. Right from my school days, I had this fear of public speaking. The moment I had to step in front of my classmates during elocution or endowment competitions, my heart would pound in my mouth and felt butterflies in my stomach and the shivering of my leg would give aches and cramps later. I didn't't face this fear of mine until I was 35 years old and once I joined the school as a teacher, the class sessions started dissolving the fear but still, I knew it was not completely gone. I decided to do all the things that scared me the most. I called up my psychology professor, asking her to invite me when there is a need to give a speech to the students on any given topic. She did call me the very next month to address the final year students and their parents about "My life's journey so far after my graduation". I felt honored but I was shivering inside like so very badly. Still the day came and I was determined to face my fear. My voice trembled once

I began addressing the crowd but later as time ticked by I was able to deliver a 30 minutes speech. The moment I completed my speech, I did feel like I did the unbelievable and a wave of happiness swept through me for the next few days. Even after the big day, I wanted to make sure I didn't have any bits of fear left behind, so I voluntarily took up more opportunities like taking up an introductory speech about the chief guest at school functions. I did find an opportunity to speak and motivate the 10th board exam students. This session went on for 120 minutes. Later I was out of my fear completely and started addressing larger crowds like college students during SHARP MEET 2019 on the importance of happiness, how to sustain happiness, the importance of starting the day in the right way and living in the moment. My bold move to face my fear was the foundation for my future workshops and I found the real ME, the hidden potential in me to lift and brighten someone's day with my words. Once in a while in our life, we need to push ourselves to our limits because everyone else is busy with their life. If you need a change you have to step up and speak up for yourself. I did and here I am today able to find the meaning and purpose of my life and live every moment with complete bliss to be happy and keep the people around me happy too!

The second occasion where I faced my fear was when we had gone on a vacation to Bangkok with family. We were taken to an island to try the parasailing ride. Kandharaj had already tried before and so he didn't want to try again. Now I was forced to try but the sight of people being lifted into the air gave me terrible fear. The previous week I had a session with 8th-grade students on the topic of fear and I felt like I was not eligible to take the class when I myself wasn't facing my fear. I asked my husband to pay for the ride and was waiting for my turn with fear and nothing other than fear. It was my birthday and my girls were talking among themselves, "What if mom lands in the water and we lose her?"

"OMG that was the last straw and I couldn't take it anymore,"

But my turn arrived and the life jacket was wrapped secure and the person in charge gave me instructions to run a few steps on the ramp and jump into the water. I said "WHAT?!!"

He told me the speed boat would pick up speed and I would lift into the air. I still can feel what I went through inside me but I did face my fear. The moment I ran over the ramp and jumped, I was in the air, really high and my family was waving to me and they looked like tiny creatures. I screamed "wooooohooooo" high up there and appreciated myself

"Good job Suma! You did it!"

The view and the feel of the parasailing were commendable and I was glad I didn't miss the beautiful moment and experience in my life. I invited my fear and looked right into its eyes. The fear was totally gone. Just a moment of courage gives you so much and so never miss the chance when the situation arises. You may note down your list of fears and have them as a bucket list. Start meeting each fear one at a time and see who you really are, find yourself. Fear is just a false cloud that stops you from becoming bigger in life. The whole world is becoming better leaving you behind. Pull yourself and face your fear NOW! Good luck mate :)

38. INSTANT HAPPINESS

Instant happiness means something that as soon as it is done gives warm fuzziness. Satisfaction and happiness are the results. It is a must for you to know what activities would make you feel happy immediately after you do them. Those activities are your life savers during stormy days. They can give you instant happiness no matter the situation or pain you may be in. Activities that give instant happiness are like lighthouses while stuck in a rough sea when it is dark everywhere and you can't see anything. Like how lighthouses guide you safely to the shore, activities that give instant happiness can help you look at the problem at hand from a different paradigm, calm you down instantly and give you the confidence to handle the issue in a better way with a better mindset.

Instant happiness is one of the topics in my journal therapy that I teach my students. The frequently asked question in the classroom is,

"How do I know what gives me instant happiness?"

Any activity that makes you forget the time and you might be working for hours together without getting tired is your instant happiness. You are in the flow and feel like doing more. When you work on something and get lost, forgetting where you are, what is happening around you, and how many hours have passed by since you started working is the key to finding instant happiness. Can I get instant happiness from people? Yes! A few people who can give you emotional support, who can understand you better, maybe soulmates. They are people to whom you can turn over for instant happiness, to pep you up and make you cheerful immediately. I have this habit of calling up my bestie when I feel down. It would be a short call or a long one and I would be the one to talk all the while and the response from the other side would only be empathctic listening. I would have regained myself again by the time I close the call.

It is very important to gain and have such people in your life to keep your happiness scale in check. Have a list of your instant happiness, not just one or two. Your instant happiness could even be your work or workplace. The mornings at home could have been so bad but the moment you step into your workplace and meet people, you would get latched to the people and place that... only when it is time for you to return home, you realize how happy you have been in spite of the big problem that happened that morning. That is instant happiness too! Instant happiness is got from people, places or activities. I know where

I can turn to for immediate lift or happiness. My mom's call,

my bestie, coffee with music, painting, reading books, yoga, working with children, time spent with my students, bedtime stories with my children, or time with my furry pet babies Fudge, Cinder, and Loki.

GUIDE TO INSTANT HAPPINESS:

1. As far as I have experienced, **being positive** makes one more resilient, attractive and boosts immunity. So less pain, fewer colds, less sickness, and better sleep. Make it a point to increase the count of positive emotions per day however bad your day may be. One positive emotion can lead to another and that keeps you in an upward spiral of positivity. Look out to find the good in any situation to keep the flow of positivity. Monitor and remove all negative weeds growing up like

   "My relationships fail. Those whom I love leave me anyway."

   "I am not capable of anything or I can't do anything on time."

   Have a few healthy distractions to jog, run, swim or play any sport.

2. You have to be **brave** enough to face all the issues that rise up in your life. Try everything that you have never done before because in the end, people regret having not done things. Being brave and taking a step forward not only motivates you but makes you feel worthy and happy.

3. Instant happiness is gained from **meditation** as we can manage our stress and reactions. You will be able to recover quickly from any disturbing people or days. Meditation teaches you to realize you are upset, helps you let go of negative thoughts surrounding your mind, deal with the issue calmly, sort it out and let go of it.

4. Loving-kindness has been the magical key in my life for immediate bliss since it has a major part to do with relating to ourselves kindly and then with others. It spreads a beautiful feeling of kindness, warmth and gentleness. You needn't worry and think if you have these qualities in you, just like how an actor takes up new roles, feel yourself become them.

5. No matter how positive you may be, all of us are touched by **pessimism**. What is pessimism? It is the state of expecting or believing that bad things will happen and that something will not be successful. In fact, you can use your pessimism to deal with the same by being a defensive pessimist and expecting the worst and rehearsing in your mind how things might go wrong. It is one handy skill and you will have to imagine what could go wrong in a situation by giving attention to specifics. By giving attention to things that might go wrong, it helps people to focus on what they could do to prevent the mishaps they imagine. This strategy prevents anxiety from intervening with what you want to complete. People who have anxiety find this method effective enough to handle their day.

Let me explain with an example. A student is to appear for his exams and is anxious about it. Becoming a defensive pessimist he would then imagine finding hard questions, or taking down the test and being unable to remember anything. This negative thinking helps one to know what they should do to prevent bad things that have played in their mind from actually happening. Well this method helps you in two ways... it motivates you to focus on the action rather than your anxious feeling and it also operates to plan effective action. This is one similar method used by counselors to help anxious people or those who have procrastination or lack motivation.

6. Activities that make you happier or keep you in a state of flow could be your **calling.** Spend more time with your family, go on holidays and vacations. Have goals in life but remember that you have to enjoy the journey and not the result. If you feel like your work is stressful and it is not your calling but you look at your job as a source of income, seek a noble purpose outside work like teaching, contributing to a cause, or charity, or just see if you can feed anybody hungry! Do things that make you happier. Find activities that completely engage your attention like singing, dancing, painting, pets, gardening, driving, etc. Happiness is something you can achieve directly or instantly. You will need work, love and a connection to something bigger.

7. Learn to master the degree of happiness. There are a few activities that happy people do naturally and they will give you instant happiness. Pick activities that would keep you in the flow like exercise, mindfulness, forgive, write down your feelings, make time for friends, practice loving kindness, don't compare and visualize a future to draw what you want in life and practice gratitude.

39. HAPPINESS AND SIMPLE THINGS

You are a pro if you can seek happiness in all the simple things in life by enjoying everything that you do mindfully. Do not engage in so many thoughts at the same moment. Don't stress yourself by thinking about waking up kids, feeding them breakfast and sending them to school on time while you are in-between your morning meditation, exercise or yoga. Do one at a time and give your complete self to what you are doing in the given moment. Seeking happiness in every simple thing will sooner become a habit.

Happiness could mean different things to different people. It could be a candle light dinner, curling up with a good book, baking, riding bicycle, walking your dog, view from terrace, nice walk, Sunday's in pajamas, doing nothing but relaxing on the couch, time spent with kids, playing madly with them, a new leaf in your indoor plant, feeling the breeze on your forehead, first drop of rain on a very hot day, running your fingers through the leaves and plants in your garden, relishing the taste of your favourite food or drink by enjoying every bit of it with gratitude, seeing the smile on your loved ones face, clean work station, not having to cook for tomorrow, greeting a stranger, trying new food, watching sunrise and sunsets, happy tear moments, rainbow after rain, observing your breath, flowers blooming, waking up every morning, fresh sheets on your bed, extra time in shower when you have free time, long phone conversation with someone you haven't spoken for a while, watching the rain, sitting cozy in your home, nice long stretch to begin the day, laughing uncontrollably over silly things, a smell you love, petrichor.. the smell outside after the rain has stopped, long hug from someone you care, pulling your feet inside the warm sheet, moments alone, holding hands with someone you love, eating breakfast in bed, playing a game you used to play when you were young, extra five minutes to sleep in bed, receiving flowers, eating out, trying a new recipe, gesture of support from family and friends, time at home when it is tidy, small victories, warm cup of tea on a cold evening, watching the steam rise from your coffee mug, sharing. The list is endless and life has given us many more things to enjoy!

The thirst for happiness should never seize and make it a point to be mindful of whatever you are doing. Mindfulness keeps you in flow and flow makes one happier. When you find it difficult to be happy for a few days, never hesitate to create your happiness. You can't expect someone to come down all the way to make you feel happy again. Sometimes we are the only one we have got for ourselves. You are your priority and it is your duty to check your happiness scale every now and then to make sure it doesn't dip.

40. CONNECT WITH YOUR INNER CHILD

Happiness is discovering the child in you. It is okay to act silly and be playful. One can't always behave like an adult, it is boring. We need some adventures, be it silly or funny but it does add to the happiness. You would have heard people say,

"Look how silly he behaves. He hasn't got out of his childhood yet."

Most of us who are parents and also our parents would have told the same,

"Act your age and don't be childish."

That is exactly where we lose our happiness and our happiness is shut behind bars. We are expected to behave for our age that at one point we forget how to keep ourselves happy!

Research suggests that while children laugh 300-400 times a day, an adult laughs only 17 times. Society, teachers, and parents consciously or unconsciously suppress our laughter and we stop being ourselves as we step into teenage and adulthood. The main reason for my happy self is that I keep my inner child alive. The little girl inside me is just the same as she was and she is the one who pulls me out of sad days. Your inner child plays a vital part to keep you lively, bubbly and cheerful. My family members know how silly I am at home… how childish I behave, crack jokes and roll on the floor just like one insane person, how I cheer, whistle and enjoy a few scenes and dialogues while watching movies, poke, tickle or hit my kids and run away and they would run behind to catch me. What fun it is to be a child even when you are in your 20's, 50's, or 80's!

Let us have a small test to find out how "adult-like" you have already become. When was the last time you wore a dress for your own comfort? When was the last time you ran into the rain to enjoy every drop of it? Did you sing aloud just for you when people were around? Did you join a child to play in the heap of wet sand to feel the wet sand and create mud cakes? When did you get on a giant wheel or merry-go-round without being accompanied by a child? How often do you laugh at a joke that just happened or an old one, without being conscious of what would others think? When did you last eat the ice lollies and cotton candy and get the color on your lips and cheeks?

You and I are struggling deep down inside of us to do something funny and silly to get away from our adult life. But only a few of us have the courage to do so. Break your fear and try as many silly things as u wanted to do.

Let us go deep into yourself to hunt for that hidden child. Try to recall some pleasant memories from your childhood and try to relive them as you read further. Gradually get yourself away from this stressful adult life and its commitments. Focus and enjoy the innocence and freedom of childhood days.

Visualize yourself surrounded by your loved ones as a school goer, you can hear the sound of your pets that you grew and feel the texture and see the color of your dolls that you treasured. Try to hear your mom or dad's voice calling out your name, do you see your grandma serving her most delicious meal? Feel the taste of your granny's food on your tongue and I am pretty sure you get the food's aroma by now. Watch yourself interacting with your family members, watch yourself with your playmates in the neighborhood or school, and notice the lively self and fun you have playing and enjoying. Remember your childhood face filled with innocence. Those tiny eyes, nose, mouth, tiny hands and fingers. There you are into your childhood days, back again. Visualize yourself running free from all chains, no one is calling you back and you have no destination to reach.

Now, you would have been able to reach and touch your childhood. If you were not able to reach your inner child or recall a happy childhood, well that is a serious issue and that is probably affecting your adult life. Maybe you have some emotions unresolved or childhood traumas that you have to work on before it pulls you down further or hinders your future happiness.

Childhood will never come back but we can always travel back to it. Every now and then when life is so hard on you, it is the best way to visit your inner child and find yourself back again. Never think about your age, just have all the fun and you get old only when you stop having fun. Life is all about being happy, funny and silly. Don't have any hard and fast rules in life, become a child again and keep the little boy or girl inside you alive forever to keep your happiness alive too.

41. RESILIENCY

Resilience is the ability to get back to your normal self, the ability to bounce back. Like how the tall grasses in the woods bend and sway in the storm, you should have the capacity to bend without breaking. Psychological association's definition of resilience is

"The process of adapting well in the face of adversity, trauma, tragedy, threats and even significant sources of stress such as family and relationship problems or workplace and financial stress. "

In other words, resiliency is the way we respond to stress. Resilient people do practice optimism. Sometimes when you keep telling people,

"Don't worry, things will be okay"

It's gonna hurt them. You should learn to practice grounded optimism when things are not okay. Grounded optimism means when things are not okay you have to look for similar situations and how you got a different outcome. We are looking for proof from the past. Optimistic people like me have good planning, I plan it well and then execute. I set my goals and do everything to accomplish them. I focus on the present moment so that I don't worry about the past or future. I don't worry about the future but plan for it. I never worry about the past because I very well know I can't change it. Never have grudges, anger or worry about the past. If you do, you are being pulled behind and wouldn't be able to enjoy the present or plan for your future. Worrying about what has already happened is a waste of time.

Resilient people are also the ones who face their fear. It is okay to feel fear and there is nothing wrong with it. If you have noticed well while facing fear one would either go to fight mode or flight mode. When a wild animal approaches you, you would either prepare to fight the animal or save your life by fleeing from the place. Facing fear would bring far more opportunities that you never knew you had. It is okay to get spiritual and get emotional support when you face fear and you can also talk to your friends and family and get their support.

If you want to be a resilient person, well you must know the difference between right and wrong. Make it a point to only choose the right thing always. Knowing what to do is part of a moral compass and to do it right you should put yourself in another person's shoes. If you can help someone without expecting anything in return, then you are resilient. Be who you are and create your own moral values. If you try to be someone else, you lose yourself and also your happiness.

It is okay to taste a bit of spirituality to be resilient. Did you know that religious people are more resilient and can deal with difficult situations better? If you practice meditation, you are connecting with some energy bigger than you and improving your overall wellbeing, happiness and resiliency. Yoga connects our mind and body and that increases our spirituality level too. Anyone who practices forgiveness is the happiest and the one to be in peace since forgiving reduces the burden on your shoulder. Of course religious rituals, prayers and chanting have their own ways to improve your resiliency. If you are not religious, you may practice yoga, meditation and mindfulness to increase your spirituality.

Some daily habits can boost the resiliency level gradually. You may write three good things that happened by the end of each day and create a gratitude habit. Practicing mindfulness in all ways like mindful talking, walking and listening helps you to focus on the present moment. Meditation is the key to resiliency. I have created a space for meditation where I start my day to connect with my inner self. Despite the turbulence outside in your world, through meditation you can stay grounded and in a calm peaceful state always.

The first and foremost predictor of happiness is relationship. Social support protects you from physical and mental illness. We will discuss more of this topic in the next chapter.

42. MY SOCIAL SUPPORT AND COUNTABILITY PARTNER

It is important to find a countability partner, who can help you achieve your goal and improve your well-being by increasing your resiliency level. You might want to do regular exercise by waking up early every morning but you tend to be lazy, well then look for someone you can trust as your countability partner, someone who can help you reach your goal. I observed my dad and his best friend Johnson as countability partners when I was in 5th grade. In spite of their age and the need for physical fitness they didn't commit to early morning walks. Maybe they didn't have an urge or motivation to begin every single day with walks. They trusted each other as their countability partners that they use to ring up one another by 5 a.m. Those were the days they only had access to landline phones. My dad use to call his friend first and by the end of three rings, he would close the call. My dad would get three rings back from his friend to confirm he is awake too. Even before sunrise, they would meet at the joggers club. My dad says even though at times when he felt lazy or sleepy to take a walk, the phone call would be a push because someone is awake and getting ready and that they should also start their day to meet up on time and also not to make the other person wait. He also added he would not stay awake late in the night to avoid ruining his friend's walk routine too. My dad has always had a great support group and more than one countability partner that, right from 1985 and till today 2022 he goes to the joggers club for a walk followed by a game of tennikoit.

Social support is gained from your partner, your friends, your family, your coworkers and importantly from strangers. Saying hello to someone in the queue or helping some homeless people makes you even happier. One morning we didn't have spinach for cooking and I heard a vendor selling spinach in the street. I called out to him through the window and he stopped his vehicle. I called out to him, "Spinach! Please wait".

My elder daughter Isha, who was having her breakfast laughed since I had named him "spinach". After buying the spinach I didn't fail to ask him his name. He replied with a smile on his face that his name was "Alaghan".

It's a Tamil name that means a beautiful person both in and out. I told him, "You have a beautiful name indeed." He took some more time to pull the conversation and told, "Alaghan is the name given to the first male child born and if it is a girl, she would be named "Ponnuthaayi". I could see the smile in his eyes and the wrinkles on his face told his ages of hard work and struggle. Those 2 minutes of conversation did make me happy and him happy too. As I collected the spinach and walked to my home I felt like I was much happier and started my day well. How could a stranger make you happy? A stranger just did by making my day :)

Have you thought about who is there for you and who can help you when you get into a tough situation? Who will help you when you lose your job? Who will take care of you when you are in a hospital? If your answer is none, well it is high time you really work hard to care for and take care of people so you could have someone to count on sometimes when you really need them.

The best way is to have a social support group and help as many people as you can. When you need help, your social support group will be there for you because you were there for them when they needed help. Let me suggest you few ways to increase your social group. I dedicate a part of the day or weekend to making phone calls. My bestie has this routine of making a call while driving back home from work. It is the need to be connected to people in spite of the busy routine you might have and in fact, few minutes of call or conversation makes the day better for both. Scheduling several meetings, walks in the park, lunch or dinner with friends and students is my way of increasing my social support. I walk around to say hello or share some kind gesture during my work at school. The break time was quite the best time to go down and meet all the students. Those quick hellos and bear hugs with students brimmed me with energy and also pepped up the young minds for the next class or the whole day. Reach out to people for no reason but to reach out.

I didn't have a countability partner during my childhood or adulthood. Somehow when I am 42 years old, I have one incredible countability partner Rishi Varman. One person whom I can always trust and count from my support group. We count on each other when we lose track of our fitness schedule or healthy diet. The last call made by Rishi Varman was in the middle of the night at 11:45 p.m. He needed some help to wake him up early the next morning since more than ten days had gone by eating outside food and also without his gym and walk routine. I called and woke him up the next morning and called him again by 8:30 am to check if he woke up or slept off after my call. He had finished his gym routine and was taking a walk then. He grabbed on to his early morning schedule and fitness routine again. None can be perfect always and we do stumble at times and need a hand to support and push. The countability partner takes that role. In the same way when I lose my yoga routine, Rishi never fails to motivate me by appreciating the way I take care of my health, fitness and the way I always look younger for my age. That would be more than enough to catch up with my fitness again and he never fails to check on me if I have hooked up with the routine. I can still remember how Rishi Varman (though I call him sonny) came into my life as an 11th-grade student and has never failed to leave my side ever. My heartfelt gratitude to my support group who have always been my support to travel further in my life!

<u>43. FRIENDS AND BESTIE</u>

Cramming or giving all of your love and affection to just one person is not a good choice. People who have multiple incomes are tactical and they are aware that when the first income is blocked, they have the second income to rely upon. Comparably it is a wise decision not to heap up all your love into one basket because spreading it and creating new bonds and new relationship enlarges your support group and in a way, you are designing more people to love you back. One wouldn't feel as upset about the experience of divorce or break-up when the best friend is around owing to the fact that a bestie's company diminishes the level of the stress hormone cortisol. During days when one fails to know about themselves and their real strength, a bestie never fails to show how able and sturdy one could be during tough days. The magnificent job of drawing you out of the downward spiral and tossing you back into the upward spiral is done effortlessly by a bestie! Conversation with your bestie can give you a sense of belonging and makes you feel happy instantly.

It is the need of the moment to have one person in your life to whom you can confide, reach out any time when life is difficult or during an emergency, a shoulder to lean on, shed tears on and a hand to wipe your precious tears. You really need that one person to hold you when you fall, support you when you stumble, and walk beside you even when the whole world is against you. During times when you deviate from life's path, the bestie never thinks twice to alert and warn you about the consequences you would have to face sooner. A bestie or soulmate never fails in his job to look right into your eyes and confirm your flaw. The outside world doesn't care if you are on the right track or not, but a friend cares because you mean the world to them and keep loving you in spite of your flaw, anger or the worst person you could ever be.

Having a best friend is a gift so rare that so many fail to see. Things don't feel so bad with your bestie nearby when your whole world is falling apart. The very thought at the back of your head, that assures your bestie is with you in spite of whatever happens is immense moral support. Earning one such friend for your whole life would be the huge happiness ever. If you have not tasted the happiness of friendship, well you should at least once! A call or conversation, be it a casual or serious one will reveal a bright spot for a week's time and it does have a considerable lasting effect on your well-being as well. Days and moments spent with friends are contagious in a way like celebrating their big day of achievement or promotion will put you in a better mood too. Friends and friendship come with new reasons to be happy over time. Showing up at your friend's house with their favourite food for no reason, sending a card, flowers or surprise cake on their birthday, or just a simple handwritten letter makes you both feel better.

It is not just best friends, even casual friends can uplift your mood. A co-worker who suggests a good book, or a woman you chat to in the gym might not count as close friends but they can still brighten your day. A loving and caring friend is so precious than anything else in one's life. This is exactly why my life has been the best with my one and only bestie and the 4 decades of friendship that we share. We got introduced as kinder garden mates and we have pulled together and been for each other through the thick and thin of life and stayed besties till this moment. Though he is hands full 24/7 with his duty and cases, there hasn't been one single moment I was deprived of attention and care when I needed the most. You might have many friends but only a bestie knows all your best and worst stories and has lived them with you. Thanks, Nut ;)

44. PETS AND HAPPINESS

Pets have the power to make us happy instantly. Being an ardent pet lover from my childhood, I have had the opportunity to raise so many pets like chicks, budgerigars, rabbits, cats, fishes, squirrels, and dogs. My husband and girls have always been dog lovers and I have raised each dog as my own baby. Sometimes when your family fails to welcome you home, your furry friend never fails to. Just stepping out for 10 minutes and returning does excite your pet. They spend so many hours, days and years awaiting your arrival. Their twinkling eyes and waggy tail have so much to convey. They are like children and you can confirm the same when they run towards you for cuddle and security hearing a sudden loud noise when they are scared or hurt accidentally. They do look adorable when they

don't understand sounds and language. Watching them tilt their head from side to side with cute innocence can make you the happiest person ever in this whole world. The way they try to get your attention by placing their little paws on us are moments that only dog lovers know.

Dogs pick your emotion and feelings well particularly when you are upset. They purposely make silly moves and do crazy things to brighten your mood. I have always had my dogs around that they are the ones to wake me up in the morning by placing their paws by my bedside and poking their wet nose right into my eyes. As soon as I wake up, they spring up and down in delight to start the day. My day begins with them and they are the ones who help me to start my day excellently. I am also thankful enough since they are keeping me in good mental health and very active though the day. My mind is busy getting them food on time, attending to their needs, playing, entertaining, getting them ready for walks, terrace play, car rides, beach visits and many more. Though they live with us for a very short time, they etch a deep mark in our hearts. They play a commendable role in your life to keep you happy. Their silky warm fur is cozy enough than the best comforter. Pet lovers live and enjoy the present moment naturally and in return, they are happier and have a positive outlook.

Dogs can give you a healthy lifestyle and also boost you to be an early bird. If you have struggled to get a good countability partner to start early morning walks, your pet dog could be the best partner. You have a reason to wake up, go for walk or just start your day early. Hand in hand you are helping each other to stay healthy and boost healthy habits.

Kids raised around pet dogs at home are psychologically balanced, mentally healthy and have the qualities of compassion, empathy, kindness, unconditional love and get the ability to treat every life equally be it small or big. Children who have pets are gentle and care for others deeply. My fur babies are my biggest source of happiness and they are with me for a reason to bring out the real me and the happiness which builds me every second. Thanks and gratitude to Snowy, Fudge, Cinder, Loki, Buddy, Fruit loop and Tofu.

45. DO NOT TAKE LIFE TOO SERIOUSLY

I have come across so many thoughts for the day posts and forwards on social media which would give a deep insight on the topic no matter how simple the words are framed. This is one such simple quote with a deep meaning,

"You are killing yourself for a job that would replace you within a week if you dropped dead. Take care of yourself."

- Unknown

This quote has conveyed enough to those who are working really hard to meet the ends meet and to please the boss. People are rushing behind money and work busily without taking care of their health and fitness. After having earned enough money, the day they plan to retire brings awareness that they have traded their health for the money and job. People run behind money for years and at one point when they have it, they would have lost their health. The same money that they earned toiling for years is spent on their medical expenses. Stephen Covey in his book 'The 7 Habits of Highly Effective People,' stresses P and PC. Production and production capability.

P and PC must go hand in hand to enjoy the fruit during your old age. People don't strike a balance between production and production capability always. The realization of the valid point that one would be able to progress and make more money, only when they are fit and healthy gets into their thick skull very late.

A few who do not like their job but just to make ends meet to pay rent, to pay the bills and fees for kid's education, continue to work in an unhappy environment that would get another person on the same seat the next moment he dies. Do not take life too seriously working so hard... you are losing so many beautiful moments of your life and the foremost is your own happiness.

There was one post on social media not sure if it was a true incident but it will knock sense into every woman who sacrifices their whole life and happiness for the sake of their family. Let me write it the same way I read it.

My dearest friend passed away a couple of weeks back. I gained the strength to call up her husband who wouldn't know to survive even a second without my friend's assistance. I was sure the whole family would be struggling hard without her around since she was the one to cook and get 3 healthy meals on the table, the one to teach her children and help them cope in academics and such a caring daughter-in-law who took care of her bed-ridden in-laws who had health issues. Though I expected a sad hello from the other side, my friend's husband sounded cheerful. I asked if things are getting better. He told that things have fallen in its place already with the appointment of a new cook who can cook anything for the whole family, a caretaker stays at home to take care of the kids and their studies, a nurse stays with the bedridden in-laws 24/7 to attend to their needs. And he also added he has taken badminton classes every evening and he just came home after finishing a match. After closing the call, I sobbed so badly. In spite of my friend having sacrificed her whole life, happiness and time, her place was replaced by someone in no time by paying extra money. She refused all the friend meetings since she had to cook and take care of her in-laws. She didn't join her parents and brother's family for a long trip since her children had their exams going on and they needed her. In no time she was replaced by someone else and wished she could have found more time for herself and enjoyed a bit for her own self with her parents, friends and her circle.

I was bitterly angry but realized that is the plight of so many women. I didn't wait a moment to forward the post to all the groups and people I knew. It did make a lot of sense. Never force yourself, stretch and pull yourself to meet ends meet at home or even at the workplace. Do anything at ease and without stress, it is okay… you needn't be in a hurry. You are precious and every moment of on-time pressure makes you go nuts and brings in more wrinkles and grey hair for your age. When your kids are late to school, that's okay! Things wouldn't change just because you hurry up and push them to school on time. They would be on time to school only when they realize it all by themselves. I would keep calm even when it is time for the school bell, they would be late to school, get punished and later realize to be on time on their own. See! It happens! Why do you want to put your health at stake? I have been there and felt my heart throb while walking back to the car after leaving my kids at school. In fact, I would realize I hadn't taken a breath at ease right from the time my kids woke up and until they entered the school premises. I didn't have anyone to tell me this stress will eventually catch up with my health. I request all the young mothers and people not to take life too seriously. Every moment of your life should be etched with happiness and you deserve it.

Also clubbing some positivity during a stressful time is handy and learning to look for something good during tough situations like when you are stuck in traffic, it means you have more time to listen to your favourite songs or make calls to people whom u always wanted to stay in touch with. If you miss the route to a place, well it is an opportunity to find new places. Life is a pleasant one to enjoy and it is you and me who make it tough.

Relax, Breathe, You still have time!

First I was dying to finish high school and start college.

And then I was dying to finish college and start working.

And then I was dying to marry and have children.

And then I was dying for my children to grow old enough for a school so I could return to work.

And then I was dying to retire.

And now, I am dying and suddenly I realize I forgot to live.

-   Anonymous

<u>CONCLUSION</u>

Happiness is different for each one of us, but we have one thing in common... it is the search for happiness. Spending each day connecting to what means happiness to us makes one live life more completely. But the fast life and trendy world make us lead a life that lacks our birthright. Stress and anxiety distract and take over our life. Utilizing happiness as a tool to win over people and situation is the secret key. The happiness hidden inside each one of us is the map or compass to connect with our purpose and the true meaning of life. Everybody's meaning of life is not the same from birth to death. It keeps changing in every stage of our life. It could be as simple as being a top scorer and graduating from your dream university during your teens and being the sweet helping neighbor spending time in the garden pulling out weeds during your 70s. Knowing the purpose and meaning of your life is like adding an extra topping to your happiness dessert. Jot down a list of what makes you happy to create your world of happiness which will be a lifesaver in the rough sea.

Knowing my life's purpose has added fuel to the fire to live my life in a more effective and complete way. My life's journey will continue spreading happiness and loving kindness until my last breath. I have laid all my targets and activities around my life goal which is to be happy and keep the people around me happy. In a way, my happiness and goals are interlinked and the result is quick and perfect! Targeting happiness could be the meaning of your life too! Your contagious happiness wave could make someone's day or even life! None have the right to seize your birthright from you and never trade your happiness.

Being a seeker of happiness, I will continue to seek it in every bit and piece of my life, as my life has exposed the secret of happiness which is to enjoy the journey and not to wait for the destination. Life is such a beautiful miracle viewing it through the happiness glass. It is okay to be selfishly happy because we know what our life is in this birth. The next birth is yet to come and you never know where you would be born, who will be your parents, your sibling, your life partner, children, friend, best friend, colleague or neighbor. You were strung together as a family for a reason and who knows you wouldn't have the same family and people again. Enjoy what you have in this moment… the people and the blessings you have been given.

Any kind of relationship should multiply your happiness and not make you feel like you are stuck in life. Go around caring for people with unconditional love as long as you live here and make your life worthy enough. We are still here much alive on this planet to work and create the best next birth by protecting every being from harm and danger. It is such a rarity to be born as a human being and so make it a point to live as one too. Time is ticking away so, act now, change now, realize the power inside you, be the change, make the change, love and care for people around you and live every single moment brimming with happiness.

Being a bookworm myself, while reading the last few pages of any book I can feel the handcuffs binding me with the book, pages, words and the author. I would wish if more pages can be added magically to continue reading. It is pure credit to the author and also a sign that it is one valuable book as a life changer. If at all you feel the same having reached the last page of this book, do reach me with your valuable feedback and comments on my page instagram.com/suma_kandharaj

May your life be filled with the ceaseless happiness wave!

Love and prayers,

Suma